Why I Triple Text:

A Guide for Understanding Your Borderline Personality Disorder Diagnosis and Improving Your Relationships

ALEXIS SANDS

Name: Sands, Alexis, author

Title: Why I Triple Text: A Guide for Understanding Your Borderline Personality Disorder Diagnosis and Improving Your Relationships / Alexis Sands

Volume: One

Description: First Edition

ISBN: 9798692776624

© 2020 Alexis Sands

All rights reserved. This book or parts thereof may not be reproduced in any form, stored in any retrieval system, or transmitted in any form by any means—electronic, mechanical, photocopy, recording, or otherwise—without prior written permission of the publisher, except as provided by United States of America copyright law.

The content provided herein are simply for educational purposes. Every effort has been made to ensure that the content provided in this book is accurate and current for my readers at publishing time. This book is not intended as a substitute for diagnosis and/or treatment from a mental health professional. The reader should consult a licensed psychiatrist or psychologist regarding matters related to their mental health. I am not a psychologist. No liability is assumed for losses or damages due to the information provided. You are responsible for your own choices, actions, and results.

Acknowledgments

I want to extend gratitude to my psychology professors for their role in shaping my conceptual understanding of personality disorders. Early on they instilled in me a compassionate approach as well as the enlightened mindset that treatment is possible.

I would also like to thank all of the individuals with borderline personality disorder who have shared their experiences, struggles, and personal stories with me. Without their candid and courageous openness, this book would not have been possible.

Special Acknowledgements

I would like to extend a special thanks to Borderline YouTuber Glo of Glo's Life for sharing her personal experiences to contribute to this book. Her channel provides relatable videos on topics affecting people with BPD, such as splitting, dissociation, and many more. As a mental health advocate, she aims to show other borderlines that they are not alone by talking openly about mental illness.

Glo and I have begun working together to help end the stigma associated with BPD. Our collaboration is in the early stages, yet we ultimately aim to create an outreach program to help borderlines in need who lack mental health resources. Look for amazing progress in the near future!

Subscribe to *Glo's Life*

https://www.youtube.com/c/GLO'sLife

TABLE OF CONTENTS

Preface   *6*
Introduction   *9*

CHAPTER ONE   13
BPD Criteria A.1.

CHAPTER TWO   35
BPD Criteria A.2.

CHAPTER THREE   69
Treatment Options

CHAPTER FOUR   83
Coping Strategies

CHAPTER FIVE   103
Coping Strategies
And Communication
Techniques

CHAPTER SIX   117
Improving Interpersonal
Relationships
Worksheets

Conclusion   *149*

About the Author   *151*

References   *152*

PREFACE

I'm Alexis Sands, own voices author of the *Blurred Borders* fiction series. I was diagnosed with borderline personality disorder (BPD) after going full-on *Girl, Interrupted* over twenty years ago. Since that time, I have experienced progress and setbacks as well as participated in several different types of treatments.

I have bachelor's degrees in psychology and in education. Not only have I volunteered at a crisis hotline and worked in a group home for teenage girls with behavioral and psychiatric issues, but I've also been a patient at a behavioral health hospital. Over the years, I've read countless books, empirical research studies, and journal articles on BPD and mental illness.

In true borderline fashion, my life has been filled with a mishmash of eclectic life experiences. I've spent as much time in clubs as I have in academia. My relationships–both romantic and those with my 'favorite person'–have been messy, amazing, and a few terrible from the gate. All have been intense and complicated, but always brimming with passion. I've been in several long-term relationships but I've also lived the single and fabulous life for long stretches. In essence, I'm the textbook, paradoxical borderline. I've struggled with every component of every criteria, some more severe than others.

What sets my book apart is that I've drawn from my real-life experiences living with BPD and blended my first-hand perspective with a compilation of psychology knowledge. It's written for those with BPD by someone with BPD. I longed to create a realistic guide for borderlines to understand their diagnosis well enough to explain it to others and to help improve their interpersonal relationships.

Most loved ones of someone with BPD do not have a background in psychology. Most of my past partners either wouldn't have understood the terminology or taken the time to read lengthy non-fiction books on

BPD. This book is intended to simplify the complexities and decode the intricate language of the Diagnostic and Statistical Manual of Mental Disorders, Fifth Edition (DSM–5) criteria for diagnosis borderline personality disorder.

I have a plethora of half-finished self-help and therapy workbooks. Many were too long to hold my interest or too vague to make a real impact. My goal for the worksheets in this book is for them to be practical and easy to complete. They are short, specific, and therefore, a useful tool to enhance the stability of your platonic and/or romantic relationships, whether utilizing them by yourself or with a loved one.

Lastly, this book series is not meant to replace treatment from a therapist, psychologist, psychiatrist, or any other licensed mental health professional. Its designed to be used to supplement treatment, facilitate understanding of the BPD diagnosis, and to enhance communication and coping skills within your interpersonal relationships.

Introduction

Borderline personality disorder is a complex mental health disorder centered on difficulties regulating one's emotions, which leads to a pattern of unstable interpersonal relationships. With BPD, the intense fear of abandonment and of rejection is also a driving force.

Most experts believe that BPD develops because of underlying biological vulnerabilities, genetic predispositions, and/or an invalidating or abusive environment(s), or a combination of the above factors. Research has shown that people with BPD have differences in brain structure and functioning. No, this doesn't mean you have a low IQ. Think about someone with epilepsy experiencing seizures or a person with a brain tumor. The differences in brain functions or structures have no bearing on their intelligence.

Studies have shown higher activity in areas of the brain that control the expression of emotion and how it is experienced in people with BPD. MRI scans have revealed a difference in structure and activity in particular areas of the brain, specifically the amygdala, hippocampus, and orbitofrontal cortex.

There are strong correlations between the emotional instability, impulsivity, and decision-making in borderlines and their brain chemistry (Brambilla, et. al., 2004). Relevant psychology research also evidences consistent data associated with the neurotransmitters oxytocin and serotonin and their role in the BPD (Herpertz, et. al., 2001). Please be aware that my explanations are condensed and simplistic versions of the physiological psychology research that show how the various components of the brain effect certain aspects of BPD.

My primary purpose in overviewing relevant brain research is to communicate how a borderline personality disorder diagnosis is NOT your fault. It's critical that you and your loved ones grasp that you did not cause this disorder. Blaming someone for having BPD is like blaming a diabetic for not being able to make their body produce insulin at optimal levels.

HOW THE BOOK IS ORGANIZED

This book–and each subsequent volume in the series–will break down the intricate language from the Diagnostic and Statistical Manual of Mental Disorders, Fifth Edition (DSM-5) criteria for BPD. Please keep in mind that the symptoms are interconnected to one another, which leads to the complexity, and often misdiagnosis of personality disorders.

The beginning chapters in each volume begin with an explanation of the targeted criteria, as outlined in the DSM-5. This book, volume one of this series, focuses on criteria A. In my own words, I'll explain what it means by describing the meaning of the psychological terminology. Next, real-world examples of what symptoms look like in daily life are provided. Examples include actions, behaviors, thoughts, and/or verbal statements. The subsequent chapters explain other criteria sub points, treatments, and coping strategies.

The last chapter contains workbook style pages, with space to write down symptoms, reactions, or triggers that cause the most conflicts or problems in your interpersonal relationships. You, beautiful borderline, can utilize the pages to identify behaviors, reactions, or internal thoughts to set goals for yourself in how you interact in your relationships, either on your own or with your loved one.

If you are working with another person, both parties should discuss which management strategies work best for their personal circumstances, daily schedules, and/or life situation(s). At the bottom of each worksheet there is a *check progress* section to assess how well the attempted coping strategies worked. Sample worksheets and extra worksheets copies are included as well. The intention is not for worksheets to be filled out once, which is why there are multiple blank copies.

Building healthy relationships and trying different coping strategies is a work-in-progress. However, this book series will not elaborate on figuring out the underlying causes of your BPD diagnosis. My goal is to deepen your understanding of what the criteria means and how the symptoms play out in real life. I also aim to provide realistic coping strategies to facilitate developing and maintaining healthy interpersonal relationships in the present.

CHAPTER ONE

BPD Criteria A.1

This chapter focuses on explaining letter **A, sub points 1.a and 1.b** from the DSM-5 criteria diagnosing borderline personality disorder (shown below). To meet the criteria for diagnosis, impairments in individual functioning and self-image should be consistent over time and present in various situations (American Psychiatric Association, 2013).

*A. Significant impairments in **personality functioning** manifest by:*

*1. Impairments in **self-functioning** (a or b):*

***a. Identity:** Markedly impoverished, poorly developed, or unstable self-image, often associated with excessive self-*

criticism; chronic feelings of emptiness; dissociative states under stress.

b. Self-direction: *Instability in goals, aspirations, values, or career plans.*

Okay, so you've read that and may be thinking, *What the actual fuck?* Or you, beautiful borderline, understand it, but have no idea how to communicate its meaning to your loved ones. Or you're thinking, *I'm so stupid. Why can't I explain this? Oh, just forget it!*

Before your inner monologue runs amok, filling your head with negative thoughts, be aware that BPD is one of the most misunderstood, misrepresented, and misdiagnosed psychiatric disorders–even amongst mental health professionals. To me, BPD is the psychiatric version of lupus, in that the continuum of symptoms vary so much in occurrence and intensity from person to person. I've felt the shame from the stigmas perpetuated by misrepresentations of BPD in pop culture. I hope my book series has a profound impact on ending the stigma by breaking down stereotypes and making the complexities more relatable.

In the *Examples* sections, you may notice certain behaviors, thoughts, responses, or statements on multiple lists. This is due to the nature of the interconnectedness of the symptoms, which lends itself to many of the emotional reactions and thinking patterns overlapping. The end of each section includes a notetaking page. I encourage you to stop, reflect, and write down symptoms that you have difficulty managing or main points.

UNSTABLE SELF-IMAGE: WHAT IT MEANS

Lacking a stable sense of identity means that someone with BPD may change their hobbies, friends, beliefs, or values on a frequent basis. These may fluctuate depending upon their circle of close friends, their favorite person, or romantic partner. Due to constant criticism from themselves or others, they are unsure of who they truly are as a person.

Many with BPD report having no clear idea of who they are or what they believe in, often asking, *Who am I?* Picture a chameleon changing colors as they move from different leaves and trees. A borderline is like a chameleon. They change who they are–their interests, tastes in music, art, or attitudes depending on their environment or their current interpersonal relationships.

Having an unstable self-image sometimes comes across to others as acting immature. People with BPD spend a significant amount of time trying to form their individual identity. On the outside, they are appear indecisive, directionless, or unpredictable. Further, what seems like immaturity is also connected to their emotional dysregulation. In essence, a person with BPD's plight to develop a stable sense of self is overwhelming and can be exhausting. As you educate yourself and process the complexities of the symptoms, you will gain true understanding of how a personality disorder is not immaturity nor a character flaw.

Lacking a secure sense of self is directly related to why a person with BPD quits or changes jobs frequently. They are uncertain what fulfills them. This is where the self-direction impairment ties into self-image, contributing to borderlines changing their mind about what they aspire to do with their life. They are indecisive about what career path to pursue, often feeling inadequate because they haven't found their calling. They don't quit or get fired from jobs because of laziness, it's linked to their struggles with their identity. Being haunted by the feeling that something is missing or a lack of personal contentment catalyzes conflicts in the workplace and, in some cases, elicits resignation or termination from employment.

UNSTABLE SELF-IMAGE: EXAMPLES

- Asking yourself, *Who am I?*
- Thinking *I'm not good enough*
- Feeling confused or inadequate, especially when asked about who you are, beliefs, aspirations, and/or life goals
- Making negative statements about abilities or appearance
- Frequently changing hair color/style
- Frequently changing style of clothing/dress
- Adapting style and interests to groups of friends, blending in like a chameleon
- Changing groups of friends, favorite person, or romantic partner, seemingly without warning
- Appearing to act younger or labeled immature
- Frequently quitting, resigning from, and/or getting fired from jobs
- Changing one's major in college, excessively
- Changing hobbies, interests, leisure activities, or preference in sports on a frequent or sudden basis

NOTES

EMPTINESS: WHAT IT MEANS

Sometimes borderlines feel non-existent, experiencing feelings of **emptiness.** This criteria is one of the most confusing and abstract. The construct of chronic emptiness is under-researched and what data exists is inconclusive (Miller, et al, 2020).

To a person with BPD it feels like *something* is missing, like there's a 'black hole' or 'gap' inside of them. Describing the sense of *incompleteness* and how it feels like there's nothing inside is difficult to articulate.

They feel disconnected from themselves, others, the world, and/or to the meaning of their life. This elusive feeling worsens when coupled with sources of stress, such as a break-up, job loss, death of a loved one, or work-related stress. During periods when symptoms are more manageable, the hollow feelings may lessen, though not necessarily.

Chronic emptiness is **not** the same as depression, hopeless, or loneliness, though some research studies show a correlation between the feelings (Miller, et al, 2020). There are connections as well between emptiness and the next point of discussion, dissociation. Though the chronic emptiness experienced with BPD is not the detachment that occurs with dissociation.

This pervasive hollowness, while a separate entity, is interconnected to other symptoms. For instance, feeling like *something* is missing, but not knowing what *it* is creates a looming sense of unfulfillment. Not being able to grasp what makes you content lends itself to having an unstable image. This is why many borderlines may change career paths or interests on a frequent basis.

Having an unsettling abyss inside–that comes and goes without warning–propels a borderline to act impulsively. Desperate attempts to fill this abstract void often spearheads reckless behaviors, such as excessive drinking or substance abuse, overspending, overeating, cutting, or sexual promiscuity.

I speculate that chronic emptiness plays a significant role in the instability of a borderline's romantic relationships. Given the lack of conclusive empirical research, I can only speak from my personal experience. (I have accumulated a superabundance of evidence in my ex-boyfriend archives). Like the storm surge invading the shoreline during a hurricane, the waves of emptiness can leave you powerless. During the calm before the proverbial storm, I try to ignore the haunting sensation. Yet, I'm compelled to react, doing whatever it takes to *not* feel the hollowness.

Those with BPD experience a sudden, but overwhelming fear of being alone. If their partner had plans and was just about to head out the door when *Hurricane Hollow* made landfall, for example, the relationship is about to take a hit. The borderline is now engulfed in this terrifying sensation. Unable to explain the feeling, the borderline reacts with frantic efforts to convince the other person to stay. Often, this results in being accused of acting *too needy* or *insecure*. After being called *clingy*, an argument swells and the fear of abandonment kicks into overdrive. If these waves are crashing while the couple is physically apart, this would be another instance where excessive messages may blow up their partner's phone.

The panic-stricken efforts to *not* feel empty inside causes the borderline to hang on too tightly, either figuratively–or sometimes literally. Like in the above example, if their partner was trying to walk out the door, the borderline may try to physically block them from leaving. Other reactions may include pleading with their partner to stay or excessive crying spells and once the emotional dam bursts, it's hard to stop. They demand attention via an emotional outburst, or if the exchange has escalated, their hurt may morph into fury.

To put this in perspective, imagine a loved one has just been diagnosed with multiple sclerosis (MS). (This disease has a bewildering number of symptoms, which can present themselves in a wide variety of ways). As the neurologist explains the host of symptoms, there are a couple that don't make sense to you and your partner is having trouble finding the right words to accurately describe how it makes them feel. You probably wouldn't decide particular symptoms aren't real or simply dismiss their manifestation as excuses to get attention.

You probably won't fully grasp the ambiguous concept of *emptiness* in one sitting. It took me a while to be able to express it with words–and I love to read and write. Psychologists and researchers struggle with how to operationally define and measure it. My suggestion is to take time to process what you read about it, reflect, and revisit this section as needed.

EMPTINESS: EXAMPLES

- Feeling invisible or like one doesn't exist
- Feeling that *something* inside is missing
- Feeling like there is a hole inside
- Frantic attempts to fill the empty void:
  - Saying anything to *not* be left alone, especially by romantic partner or favorite person
  - Begging or pleading with the loved one to stay with them
  - Attempts to block or thwart loved one from physically leaving
  - Expressing anger, in words/gestures, towards the one who is 'leaving'–if together–home/restaurant/vehicle (i.e. plans, a prior obligation, wanting time to themselves)
  - Repeated (often excessive) phone calls or texts to loved ones
  - Uncontrollable, often inexplicable, crying spells
  - Withdrawing- not answering calls or responding to messages

- Isolation- not going out, socializing, or interacting with others
- Suicidal thoughts or threats
- Self-mutilation (cutting)
- Skin-picking, or other body-focused repetitive behavior (BFRB)
- Substance abuse–drinking excessively, using recreational drugs, misusing prescriptions drugs

*Suicidal ideation/thoughts, self-mutilation, substance abuse are elaborated upon in further detail in a separate volume, but if these symptoms present themselves, please seek immediate medical attention.

NOTES

DISSOCIATION: WHAT IT MEANS

Dissociation is the process of separating thoughts or emotions from one another. It's a mechanism the helps one cope with too much stress. It can last several minutes or for hours in people with BPD. In certain cases or with dissociative identity disorder (DID) or depersonalization/derealization disorder (DDD), it may last for days, weeks, or even months.

With BPD there are two types of dissociation that may occur, **depersonalization and derealization**. With both there is an underlying sense of detachment (Ross, CA, 2007). Depersonalization and derealization symptoms may occur in isolation, however, it is common for symptoms from both to present themselves at the same time.

Depersonalization is feeling a separation between yourself and your body. It's the sensation of being disconnected from yourself. People who've experienced it report that they feel like they're observing their own body from the outside, or watching themselves as if they're in a dream. Some have described not recognizing themselves in the mirror.

Derealization is a feeling of being detached from the external world, such as from other people or objects. It causes familiar things to look strange, unreal, or unfamiliar. Some that have experienced derealization describe the world around them as looking fake, foggy, or as if they are viewing it through a veil.

In my experiences, which inspired some scenes in my fiction series, I often liken it to watching myself in a movie. When I dissociated, it usually involved both depersonalization and derealization simultaneously. Reflecting back, these episodes were more prevalent when I was under duress from other stressors in my chaotic life.

One of my favorite YouTube channels about BPD is *Glo's Life*. In an excellent video about dissociation (https://youtu.be/B401CJR4CUM), Glo explains how she would dissociate by escaping into a little world that she created, in her head, whenever situations became too overwhelming. I can relate as I would often slip into my own alternate reality. Before I was aware of the concept of dissociation, I thought I'd brilliantly invented this innovative way to avoid dealing with uncomfortable feelings or awkward situations.

People with BPD may experience more episodes of dissociation when they are under stress caused by finances, work, or relationships. Also, witnessing a traumatic event, domestic violence, or the death of a loved one increases one's vulnerability to dissociation.

DEPERSONALIZATION: EXAMPLES

- Feeling like you're outside your body

- Feeling as if you're looking down on yourself from above or floating

- Feeling detached from yourself, as if you have no actual self

- Asking yourself *Who am I? Am I real?*

- Feeling a physical numbness, as if your senses have been 'turned off'

- Feeling one *cannot* control what you do or say, almost robotic

- Feeling like your body parts are the wrong size/ disproportionate or shrunken

- Looking in a mirror and not recognizing one's self

- Experiencing the sensation like your head is wrapped in cotton

- Difficulty attaching emotion to memories

- Experiencing an inability to recognize or describe emotions
- To another person, person in state looks zoned or spaced out

NOTES

DEREALIZATION: EXAMPLES

- Experiencing a distorted sense of time — the past feels recent, but recent events feel like they happened a long time ago
- Difficulty recognizing surroundings
- Perceiving your surroundings as hazy, almost dreamlike
- Feeling like you're in a movie or dream
- Feeling like a glass wall separates you from the world — you can see what's beyond but can't connect
- Experiencing the perception that your surroundings aren't real or seem flat, blurry, too far, too close
- Experiencing a distorted sense of time — the past feels recent, but recent events feel like they happened a long time ago
- Experiencing distortions in vision- like you're seeing the world through a veil or glass wall
- To another person, person in state looks zoned or spaced out

NOTES

CHAPTER TWO

BPD Criteria A.2

This chapter breaks down and explains letter **A, sub points 2.a and 2.b** from the DSM-5 criteria for diagnosing borderline personality disorder (shown below). The components of these sub points deal specifically with empathy and intimacy impairments within the context of interpersonal relationships. To meet the criteria for diagnosis, the expression of these traits should be consistent over time (American Psychiatric Association, 2013).

*2. Impairments in **interpersonal functioning** (a or b):*

*a. **Empathy:** Compromised ability to recognize the feelings and needs of others associated with* *interpersonal hypersensitivity (i.e., prone to feel slighted or insulted); perceptions of others selectively biased toward negative attributes or vulnerabilities.*

b. Intimacy: *Intense, unstable, and conflicted close relationships, marked by mistrust, neediness, and anxious preoccupation with real or imagined abandonment; close relationships often viewed in extremes of idealization and devaluation and alternating between over involvement and withdrawal.*

COMPROMISED EMPATHY/ INTERPERSONAL HYPERSENSITIVITY: WHAT IT MEANS

Empathy is *the action of understanding, being aware of, being sensitive to, and vicariously experiencing the feelings, thoughts, and experiences of another person.*

The definition is not difficult to comprehend. However, I feel the term 'compromised' muddies the waters when elaborating upon a borderline's ability to recognize the feelings and needs of others. The myth that they are selfish couldn't be further from the truth. According to a review of clinical anecdotes and relevant literature by Dinsdale and Crepsi, it was found that people with BPD don't lack the ability to understand another's feelings, but rather have demonstrated even enhanced empathetic responses in certain contexts. (Dinsdale & Crepsi, 2013). Borderlines are highly perceptive to the emotions of others, picking up on subtleties and non-verbal cues that many people miss.

The relationship between people with BPD and empathy is conflicting in nature. This is primarily attributed to their 'black and white'—also known as dichotomous or polarized—thinking patterns influence empathy. Borderlines tend to view people as 'all good' or 'all bad' or approach things with an 'all or nothing' attitude. With black and white thinking patterns, there are zero shades of grey. Such polar extremes in the way a borderline feels about a person reminds me of a quote from one of my favorite authors, Sylvia Plath. "I like people too much or not at all." Her words capture the essence of how I usually feel after meeting a new person, whether a friend or a romantic interest.

They're capable of being exceptionally loyal, caring, and empathic. Yet, due to difficulties regulating their emotions, a critical remark or harsh look abruptly changes the way they think about or categorize someone. When someone says or does something a borderline construes as hurtful, they plummet from ecstatic into the depths of emotional agony in seconds. These two opposite perspectives are paradoxical and referred to as the borderline empathy paradox (Dinsdale & Crepsi, 2013).

These swift changes in perceptions tend to come across as non-empathetic or callous. In reality what the borderline endures after a perceived insult is excruciating anguish. Their angst is so fierce that it compels them to overanalyze every scathing word that sparked the inner turmoil. The borderline obsesses over the fresh emotional wounds inflicted by the person they'd held in high regard. Therefore, they're unable to show compassion towards the once-admired person because the borderline's convinced that they pretty much hate them. This type of emotional reaction leads into the next component, **interpersonal hypersensitivity.**

Interpersonal hypersensitivity refers to how a borderline experiences emotions to a greater depth. Their intense feelings resonate longer than compared to others in similar situations. The intensity of their moods fluctuate rapidly and once triggered, they demonstrate a significantly slower return to their emotional baseline state (Linehan et al., 2014).

A borderline's reaction to a perceived insult or critical look is integral in how their hypersensitivity affects their empathy and the stability of their interpersonal relationships (Crowell et al., 2009). Once they interpret a remark as a slight or put down, it slices deep.

I could share thousands of personal examples, but I'll choose one. After I'd worked diligently on a work project, my efforts paid off. Only two others and I achieved high enough distinction to earn state recognition. The next day on the announcements, the other two names were acknowledged, but mine was not mentioned. Instantly, my eyes watered as a tornado of wrath whirled. It ruined my entire day. Logically, I comprehended it was an oversight–and not that big of a deal–but I couldn't harness control over my raging emotions. This was prior to participating in therapy; hence, from that day forward that supervisor became *persona non grata.*

People with BPD are sensitive to the way others treat them (Jackson et al., 2009). Feelings of intense bliss and gratitude flow–plentifully and freely–when someone treats them with genuine kindness and compassion. On the other hand, actual (or perceived) criticisms evoke profound anguish or explosions of anger. After an icy facial expression or minor insult, someone they once admired is instantly regarded as a grave disappointment– or possibly earning the title of arch nemesis.

It's the debilitating hurt that's challenging to communicate. There aren't enough analogies, in my opinion, to do it justice. I remember a former boyfriend rolling his eyes at me in traffic. This was a rare instance where I was the one behind the wheel, as I'm notorious for my bad driving. Anyway, the exasperated look on his face stung, down to the core.

Much later, I was able to put the gesture into perspective. But in the moment–and for hours afterwards–I couldn't contain the funnel cloud of rejection twisting inside me. *He hates me. He believes I'm worthless.* Negative thoughts ran amok in my head. Trying to brush it off takes a substantial amount of effort and time spent practicing coping techniques. Imagine pouring lemon juice straight into an open wound, that's sort of the emotional equivalent–and why it's referred to as *hyper*sensitivity.

After examining the two components of the brain, how a borderline interprets the stimuli–words or expressions of others–and why regulating their emotions is so difficult, should click. First, the amygdala processes emotions and controls how they are experienced. Second, the dorsolateral prefrontal cortex is involved with higher order processes, such as inhibition, decision-making, cognitive flexibility, and regulating emotions. People with BPD have a hyperactive amygdala and a less active dorsolateral prefrontal cortex, particularly when processing negative emotional stimuli (Schulze, et. al., 2016).

    I feel Dr. John Krystal, the editor of *Biological Psychiatry,* hit the nail on the head when he explained the concept with an easy-to-understand analogy.
Imagine that the brain was like a car. The gas pedal for emotion might be the amygdala and the emotional brake might be the dorsolateral prefrontal cortex. The current findings seem to suggest that, in borderline personality disorder, the brain steps on the emotional gas pedal. However, it does not as effectively brake or control emotions (Schulze, et. al., 2016, p. 79).

    On the surface what's deemed an overreaction, is elicited by a hyperactive amygdala. How remarks or non-verbal cues are interpreted is processed in this area of the brain (Schulze, et. al., 2016). Brain scans of people diagnosed with BPD have shown evidence of a hyperactive amygdala. According to Donegan, this higher amount of activity is linked to their emotional dysregulation and causes their 'frantic efforts to avoid real or imagined abandonment' (Donegan et al., 2003, p.1291). Hence, a borderline doesn't lack the desire to control emotional outbursts. Rather their intense emotional reactions are in response to *how* their brain perceives and interrupts the words and actions of others.

Upside of the Empathy/Sensitivity Paradox

Conversely, a borderline's sensitiveness and perceptiveness highlights their loving and creative sides. *Yah! Finally, some positive traits.* When someone with BPD loves someone, it's with every fiber of their being. Their ability to feel everything so intensely radiates.

People with BPD are intuitive and creative by nature. Contrary to media portrayal, most are deeply caring, intelligent, and introspective. While there isn't quantitative research to directly prove the prevalence of these qualitative attributes, there are studies that repeatedly report these qualities in borderlines.

For example, in PI-500, a long-term clinical study in which two-thirds of the borderline subjects were operationally defined as 'clinically well' after intensive follow ups, found evidence to support creativeness. The research indicated that BPD patients who exhibited favorable results (being well) had higher than average intelligence quotients (IQ), specifically IQ greater than

130, displayed an unusual artistic talent, and the women participants were identified as rating above-average on physical attractiveness constructs (Stone et al., 1987).

None of the current research I reviewed evaluated attractiveness. Though I found it interesting because many borderlines I've interacted with in online support groups have commented on how it seems likes everyone with BPD is really good- looking.

Another clinical study provided evidence showing that 74% of its borderline subjects displayed a special gift or talent, and found these subjects to be atypically perceptive about the feelings of others (Park et al., 1992). Replicable research shows that **gifted people exhibit characteristics, such as emotional or behavioral intensities and sensitivities, idealism, perceptiveness, asynchronies, and other complex attributes.** (Jackson et al., 2009). I believe it's vital for your self-image to embrace your unique personality traits. Every part of it doesn't need to be 'fixed' and part of what causes your darkness is also what makes you shine.

A host of artists and creative types–painters, sculptors, musicians, writers, poets, dancers, actresses/actors, comedians, chefs– have (or were rumored to have)–borderline personality disorder. It's my opinion that the hallmark emotional intensity and fluctuating moods kindle the creative fires. Channeling your angst into artistic endeavors is a positive way to manage negative thought patterns. Also, it's a constructive way to redirect anger or anxiety and contributes to you developing a stronger sense of self.

If you've heard that people with BPD never stick with anything long, it isn't always the case. While borderlines can be chameleons, changing styles and interests to those around them, this won't be the case with every endeavor. For instance, I've changed my hair color and career choices too many times to count. However, I've written and published two novels, along with this book. Thus, writing piqued my interested and never wavered. If you haven't found your passion or talent, don't worry you have a gift, you just haven't opened your package yet.

You'll notice the next section is flooded with paradoxical examples of thoughts and behaviors. *Why is everything with BPD a paradox?* I've stayed up late too many nights overanalyzing the irony of BPD's dichotomous nature. *I want unconditional love so badly, so why do I push it away? How can I go from ecstasy to agony so quickly?*

I gave up dwelling upon it. The fundamental cause of the emotional dysregulation is grounded in my brain structure and function. I've learned to manage my emotions and other symptoms, and to accept setbacks. I cannot change the nature of my intense and dynamic personality. And certain aspects, I have no desire to alter– it's what makes being borderline such a *rara avis*.

COMPROMISED EMPATHY/ INTERPERSONAL HYPERSENSITIVITY EXAMPLES

- Extreme emotional reaction or angry outbursts to changes in plans
- Canceling plans (to avoid perceived rejection or to avoid having plans changed on them)
- Standing up for justice, verbally or via actions, or participating in social or political activism
- Standing up for unfairness in the workplace, regardless of the consequences, and/or to point of job loss
- Angry outbursts, verbal arguments, crying spells in response to minor criticism or perceived slight
- Expressing overt happiness or elated moods after praise or compliments from a loved one
- Exhibiting strong emotional response(s) that seem too intense, not age-appropriate for situation, deemed child-like
- Ignoring/avoiding or 'cutting off' people who accuse borderline of 'acting like a child'

- Misconstruing messages or lack of immediate response as rejection or abandonment and reacting with incessant texts, calls, or begging
- Anticipating loved one's needs ahead of time
- Ability to intuitively read emotions (without being explicitly told)
- Misreading other's emotions or thoughts based off of minor cues or non-verbal expressions
- Difficulty letting go of 'toxic' relationships, i.e. not treated fairly or one that is emotionally, mentally, or physically abusive
- Showing unwavering loyalty to loved one, going above-and-beyond typical expectations to make them feel loved, cared for, or to meet their needs
- Oversharing intimate, personal information early on in a relationship
- Unable to calm down, self-soothe or stop crying in a reasonable time frame consistent with given situation
- Thinking *I'm not enough*
- Thinking *I'm too much sometimes*
- Exerting intense effort/focus on task, project, and/or creative expression, often over-achieving

- Becoming frustrated or angry, if something goes wrong with task, project, or form of creative expression
- Withdrawing or giving up on a project/task when receiving criticism (negative or constructive)
- Spending *all* available time with or giving *all* attention to a romantic partner or favorite person
- Experiencing emotional duress and intense pain if a romantic partner or favorite person doesn't return the same or desired amount of attention

NOTES

FEAR OF ABANDONMENT: WHAT IT MEANS

The fear of abandonment–whether imagined or real–lies at the heart of BPD. At the core of BPD, it's a catalyst that impacts every other symptom. It's interlinked to the fear of rejection and the emotional hypersensitivity components.

The fear of abandonment may be activated by a significant situation, like a break-up, or by something minor, like someone showing up late for a lunch date. To the borderline, the magnitude of the trigger–whether perceived or real–is irrelevant. Once stimulated, this fear becomes all-consuming. It causes an almost unbearable emotional pain often accompanied by physical pain, such as a stomachache or a tight chest.

For me, it's difficult to express how it feels when I'm convinced a partner is losing interest in me or rejects me, and thus, will soon leave me. If they don't reply to a text, explicitly praise me consistently, or express the subtlest signs of criticism, the sensation that they're pulling away seizes me. Explaining why I'm petrified in response to what's deemed *ridiculous* or labeled *overreacting* is a struggle. Attempts to reason with myself are overpowered by the acute sense of despair whirling inside me.

I don't want to humiliate myself or come across as clingy, but I cannot control the debilitating pain. The anxious energy escalates quickly, blocking my ability to focus on anything else. Panic sets in as other unexplainable fears spawn. I overthink that my partner may have been hurt, killed, or vanished due to foul play.

When I attempt to stifle my thoughts, my internal monologue runs full-throttle. My inner voice chides how undesirable, unlovable, and unworthy I must be for my partner not to show me unconditional love. My aims to voice how afraid I am and how I crave my partner's affection and reassurance that I'm loved are overshadowed by my erratic behaviors and intense reactions.

The reactions to the fear of abandonment that I described may or may not be the same for others with BPD. The specific reactions and severity will vary. However, this fear is a fault line with exponential potential to rip intimate relationships apart. If a borderline cannot convey its scope to their partner or if couples are unable to collaborate on coping strategies, then it's likely to be a substantial source of friction.

Imagine, for example, a borderline's live-in partner returns home late from work. As their fear builds, they send triple-texts and leave a slew of voicemails. Yet, the partner's phone battery had died and they'd forgotten their charger. *Today of all days.* They walk through the door to find their BPD partner in hysterics, lashing out about the lateness and unanswered messages. After a heated conversation, the partner tells the borderline to stop being so emotional and blowing things out of proportion.

After similar reactions to their fear of abandonment, such as multiple arguments, excessive number of texts, the partner becomes frustrated. The borderline senses the distance, and thus, becomes hypervigilant, always looking for signs that their partner is losing interest. Unable to self-soothe, the feelings of hollowness deepen. They feel like they are constantly waiting for the other shoe to drop, even when the relationship is going well.

Over time, this pattern causes the person with BPD to take more drastic efforts to hang onto their loved one. However, their attempts to show how much they care comes across as smothering or needy. In turn, the borderline is scathed by what they believe is their partner's thoughtlessness or lack of affection while the partner is upset at what they interpret as a lack of trust. At this point, the fear of abandonment rages until both people are exhausted from the strain of the emotional tension.

Why the borderline's innate fear of abandonment (or rejection) provokes such intense reactions is linked to their brain's physiology. The amygdala, often coined *The Holy Grail of Psychology*, plays a leading role. A human brain actually has two amygdalae, which control how one experiences emotions and perceive them in other people (Herpertz, et. al., 2001). Remember that emotional gas pedal? The amygdala plays an essential role in processing fear, how its interpreted and experienced (Schulze, et. al., 2016).

For example, the amygdala activates whenever a person experiences a 'trauma' such as rejection, fear of something, betrayal, a loss, etc. This trauma wavers on a continuum, but is always dependent upon the fight-flight-freeze (FFF) response (Schmidt, 2008). When a stimulus or trigger is encountered, a message is sent to the amygdala (from the thalamus). (Please note that I'm leaving out a significant amount of the complicated functionality of the limbic system in an effort to offer an easy-to-understand, simplified version).

The amygdala sends a message to the hippocampus and the prefrontal cortex. It links the fear response to the stimulus–the person or the event. The hippocampus and prefrontal cortex help the brain interpret the stimulus and determine whether it's perceived as a threat (Schmidt, 2008). The hippocampus is the center for short-term memory and the prefrontal cortex controls executive functions, like problem-solving, decision-making, and planning (Brambilla, et. al., 2004) Thus, it's important to consider that research studies have revealed hippocampus volume reductions (between 13% and 20%) in people with BPD, in addition to the previously discussed hyperactive amygdala (Donegan et al., 2003). This shows why they overreact and have a difficult time controlling their heightened emotional reactions.

When a person perceives a danger, whether emotional or physical, these two brain structures release hormones, such as cortisol and norepinephrine (adrenalin). These stress hormones influence the capacity of the prefrontal cortex to regulate decision-making in response to danger (Mhillaj, et. al., 2015). For instance, say you encounter a rabid dog on the sidewalk, after perceiving the threat, you make a decision to keep yourself from getting bit. You may have a flight response, and run away. Or perhaps you have a taser and react with a fight response, stunning the canine. Or perhaps you stand motionless, in hopes that Cujo will lose interest and walk away.

If the person's automatic response in the situation leads to safety, they typically spend the next few days re-telling the event, venting, or processing it in some way. This enables them to heal and the trauma cycle is completed. Soon, they return to a normal neurobiological state.

However, sometimes fight and flight are activated, but do not lead to safety. Both may have been attempted and failed, or not a viable option given the circumstances. During a home invasion, for instance, a person 'plays dead' when outnumbered by armed and erratic assailants. In this scenario, freeze kicks in to protect or modulate the (physical and emotional) pain the person is about to experience. At this point the brain releases a super-dose of endogenous opioids. These opiate-like substances–endorphins, enkephalins, and dynorphins–are produced by the body and used as neurotransmitters (Mhillaj, et. al., 2015).

The cycle of being stuck in freeze mode is like an idling engine. Over time, the incessant running causes significant emotional duress because the trauma cycle was never *turned off.* This type of anxiety underpins disorders like BPD, post-traumatic stress syndrome (PTSD), and addiction. The brain reacts in the same way to triggers in future situations. The outcome is repeated and overactive responses are elicited whenever a threat of any kind is perceived. In order for the person to heal, the incomplete trauma cycle must be addressed. To stop the overactive reactions, the source of the trauma needs to be 'worked through' or in essence acknowledged, analyzed, and adequately processed in therapy or as part of a researched-based treatment method.

In people with BPD their fear of abandonment is rooted in the fact that their fight or flight response was activated during childhood or adolescence, but did not lead them to feeling safe and secure. The initial trauma may have been physical or sexual abuse. Contrary to misconceptions, abuse isn't necessarily a causation factor. It could be any experience(s) in which the borderline didn't receive adequate emotional affirmation, such as being told to 'stop being a baby' whenever they expressed their feelings about social problems with friends, for example. Regardless of the circumstances, most borderlines did not have their emotional and/or physical needs met as a child or adolescent. The lack of security and emotional validation during critical periods of brain development causes them to anticipate future rejection, often at the slightest trigger.

Thus, whenever the borderline faces real or perceived rejection or abandonment, their brain idles in freeze mode. Once triggered, their overpowering fear takes over. Their erratic reactions are attempts to feel validated, loved, and secure–and stop the sheer fright from reeling through them over and over. I feel it's imperative that people with BPD and their loved ones understand the physiology underlying this fear to avoid blaming the borderline. To move forward and heal, the initial emotional invalidation which catalyzed their fear of abandonment needs to be acknowledged, processed, and worked through, preferably in a therapeutic setting and with their loved ones.

FEAR OF ABANDONMENT: EXAMPLES

- Thinking *I'm unlovable*
- Thinking/saying *I'm not enough/good enough/unworthy*
- Thinking/saying, *He/she/everyone hates me*
- Asking for constant reassurance, such as *Do you care? Am I important? Do you love me?*
- Becoming attached too quickly (especially with romantic partners)
- Obsessing about people leaving or rejecting
- Excessive messages or calls as a frantic effort to avoid perceived or actual abandonment
- Suddenly cutting off communication with loved one
- Breaking up with a partner to avoid them leaving
- Bouncing from relationship to relationship
- Choosing emotionally unavailable partners
- Staying too long in an unhealthy relationship
- Doubting love or anticipating rejection

- Taking extreme measures to avoid separation, such as physically blocking someone from leaving
- Sabotaging relationships to avoid rejection, whether perceived or actual rejection
- Difficulty controlling emotions–sadness, anger, or jealousy–when physically apart from partner
- Controlling behaviors or a control-freak in many areas of life
- Catastrophizing–playing out worst case scenarios
- Over-giving and sacrificing own needs to make partner happy
- Self-harm, self-mutilation, or cutting behaviors
- Impulsive or reckless behaviors, such as excessive drinking, recreational drug use, promiscuity, excessive spending, reckless driving
- Suicide threats or attempts
- With comorbidities, symptoms of other disorder(s) may intensify, i.e. increased panic attacks with anxiety disorder, heavier drinking with substance abuse disorder, changes in eating habits with anorexia

NOTES

IDEALIZATION/DEVALUATION/SPLITTING: WHAT IT MEANS

The fear of abandonment coupled with emotional deregulation springboards into **alternating between extremes of idealization and devaluation** or what is called *splitting.*

Idealization is a defense mechanism in which a person overestimates the good qualities of a particular person or thing. For example, when I meet someone for the first time, immediately I can tell if I'm going to like them. If I do like them, my feelings are not lukewarm, they are so intense they almost spontaneously combust. I tend to perch my perfect, *favorite person* on a pedestal– and they can do no wrong. Borderlines often give a person or thing exaggerated positive attributes. The over-the-top emotions exhibited with idealization are connected to the emotional hypersensitivity component.

Devaluation is the exact opposite of idealization. A comment, criticism, or facial expression may cause those with BPD to feel hurt or slighted by someone they once idealized. Based on their new perception, the borderline becomes convinced that the person is now completely flawed or lacks value. They are now viewed as having exaggerated negative qualities. In romantic relationships devaluation is prone to occurring after the initial honeymoon or exciting phase fades. When reality sets in and both partners flaws are revealed, the borderline's fear of rejection or abandonment may be triggered. Someone with BPD has difficulty recognizing and accepting that people make mistakes. In an effort to protect themselves from abandonment, the borderline's perception of their partner becomes distorted. When this happens, they tend to hone in on their negative qualities.

Their emotional deregulation intermingled with **black and white thinking** patterns cause swift shifts between idealization and devaluation. People with BPD have difficulties comprehending the complexities in human nature and circumstances. From their perspective, people or situations are perceived as amazing or horrible. Fluctuating between idealization and devaluation, they struggle to see traits or qualities that fall in between the two extremes.

This dichotomous way of thinking leads to the *splitting* **defense mechanism** as a way to cope with perceived stress and anxiety. Done subconsciously, it's how borderlines protect themselves from the emotional pain of abandonment, rejection, isolation, or loneliness.

Though people with BPD are capable of showing empathy and are insightful thinkers, when their feelings are hurt, it becomes a challenge for them to recognize paradoxical qualities.

When a borderline *splits* it means they quickly change how they view someone or something. They alternate between idealization and devaluation, bouncing from ecstasy to agony, sometimes in seconds. Splitting refers not only to their thoughts, but also their actions and words. This cycle leads to unstable relationships and if positive coping strategies are not utilized, it can devastate them. For example, imagine you are in a committed relationship. You are content, being treated well, and in love. However, your live-in partner comes home late from work. Your perception of them swiftly shifts. You perceive your partner's actions as inconsiderate and thoughtless, causing you to feel unloved.

The emotional hurt of feeling unloved intensifies and becomes so unbearable that you resort to the splitting behaviors to ease the agony. These intolerable feelings swirl with their underlying fear of abandonment. While splitting, the borderline may blame their partner for how they feel, without realizing it. They have no awareness that their feelings belong inside of them. They perceive they are being mistreated and rejected in some way. The partner on the receiving end often feels blamed or attacked. If an argument flares up, their words to defend their actions may be taken the wrong way.

As the exchange becomes heated or as similar scenarios repeatedly occur, both partners end up damaging the relationship over time. The couple becomes stuck in the cycle of splitting and defensive patterns. Both are unable to understand the other's point-of-view and cannot communicate effectively, resulting in arguments.

However, there is hope for people with borderline personality disorder. Contrary to the stigma, borderlines can have healthy and fulfilling relationships. This cycle can be stopped with awareness, communication, and the use of coping mechanisms (explained in subsequent chapter).

IDEALIZATION/DEVALUATION/SPLITTING EXAMPLES:

- Using words like *never, all, always, none, hate, love, good, or bad*
- Negative self-talk, i.e. *I'm stupid* or *I'm worthless*, often the moment something minor goes wrong
- Black and white thinking patterns, i.e. thinking if you don't score an 'A' on an English paper, you should drop the class
- Rapidly initiating relationships or becoming attached to people too quickly
- Oversharing intimate, personal details early-on in relationships
- Sending mixed messages (verbal or written), i.e. *I hate you/don't leave me, I need you/don't call me again, You don't care about me/please let's talk*
- Expressing distrust of the motives or intentions of others

- Outburst of rage (yelling insults, slamming objects, or breaking things)
- Passive reactions, such as withdrawing, or socially isolating
- Avoiding communication or giving the 'silent treatment'
- Suddenly cutting off communication with someone (leave first to avoid perceived abandonment)
- Denying feelings/emotions or projecting them onto another person
- Internalizing or 'nit picking' flaws with oneself
- Slipping into dissociative states
- Voicing extreme viewpoints on subjects, with no flexibility, leading to arguments
- Episodes of depression
- Acting out without consideration of the consequences, which leads to impulsive or reckless behaviors, such as drinking, recreational drug use, promiscuity, excessive spending, reckless driving

NOTES

CHAPTER THREE

Treatment Options

This chapter overviews research-based mental health treatment options for treating and managing BPD. No one approach has statistically significant effectiveness over another. What works for one person may not be a good match for another. Your relationship with a qualified psychologist or therapist is always an influential factor in the effectiveness of any treatment plan. If you have comorbidities- other mental health disorders- those play a role, too, in which approaches may be more appropriate.

Years ago, I began Dialectical Behavior Therapy (DBT) and found it valuable and practical- however, I didn't complete it. I had moved and it wasn't available in my new location. Psychoanalytic 'talk-therapy' has also worked for me. After reading way too much on social media and the internet about BPD going away with age, I fell into a cycle of self-shame and negative thinking. Yet, like any condition or disorder there are too many variables involved for blanket statements to hold much truth. For me, certain symptoms have lessened in severity. Through reading and educating myself, I've learned to not feel guilty about my set-backs. I've experienced large chunks of time when my symptoms have been manageable. But in-between I've made so many round-trip excursions down the rabbit hole and back that I'm the poster child for their frequent flyer club. I'll never be one of those people who brag about no longer having BPD.

    My advice to you is to figure out which approach works best for you and ignore anyone else's claims. I realized I need to continue therapy to maintain because though I give good, solid advice, I seldom follow it. In addition to determining the type of therapy that suits your preferences, finding a practitioner you trust is essential.

Types of Treatments for Borderline Personality Disorder

Dialectical Behavior Therapy (DBT)

DBT was developed by Dr. Marsha Linehan, a psychologist, at the University of Washington. This comprehensive treatment is evidence-based. It's fundamental premise is centered around a core feature of BPD, difficulty regulating emotions. The primary focus of DBT is help those with BPD understand how to recognize and control their reactions to triggers. In targeting emotional regulation, it helps borderlines apply the management strategies learned in daily life situations (Chapman, 2006).

DBT uses a combination of talking and role-playing to facilitate participants in reigning control over their emotional reactions. A combination of individual and group therapy sessions are required. Individual sessions focus on coping mechanisms and applying problem-solving skills. 'Homework' is given and provides the client with the opportunity to reflect and practice. Within the framework, therapists work with individual clients and provide validation while implementing change-oriented strategies. During the group sessions clients practice mindfulness skills, regulating their emotions, stress tolerance techniques, and role play acceptance of reality as well as interpersonal effectiveness (Linehan, 2014).

Mentalization-Based-Therapy (MBT)

    This form of treatment was founded by Drs. Peter Fonagy and Anthony Bateman, when they were psychologists at the University of London. MBT is a long-term, psychodynamic therapy, drawing its roots from Bowly's attachment theory. This approach is based on the idea that people with BPD suffer from difficulties developing adequate mental pictures of emotions, thoughts, intentions, needs, and desires. One of the initial goals of treatment is to stabilize how emotions are expressed.

    MBT places an emphasis on one's capacity to mentalize- think about thinking. One of its primary goals is to help borderlines make sense of their thoughts, beliefs, and feelings by connecting these to their reactions and behaviors. Individual sessions focus on thinking about what's going in your mind and use your awareness to develop a more balanced perspective about the thoughts of others.

MBT may also involve group and/or family therapy, but therapeutic techniques vary greatly amongst therapists. Clinical studies involving this type of therapy have shown effectiveness for clients who experience intense emotional distress that result in destructive behaviors such as aggression or self-harm. Also, it's used to treat other disorders, such as eating disorders, depression, and addiction (Bateman & Fonagy, 2009).

Transference-Focused Psychotherapy (TFP)

TFP a manualized, twice-weekly, individualized therapy based on object relations theory, which is the belief that humans are motivated by social interaction and relationships with others. This approach is based on Doctor Otto Kernberg's object relations model of BPD. TFP aims to identify problematic patterns of interaction during sessions. Also, the main focus is on the present, not the past.

The underlying premise is that your feelings about significant people in your life will be transferred onto the therapist. You react to your therapist like he/she were particular people you identified in initial sessions. Through this transference, the therapist assesses your interaction skills and uses the information to facilitate you in developing healthier relationships (Yeomans, et al., 2015).

With TFP, your relationship with the therapist is critical to effectiveness. Therapeutic techniques such as clarifying internal states to help understand and contain emotions requires a great deal of trust and time. Also, the therapist rarely instructs you on what to do, doesn't give opinions, and is NOT available outside of therapy sessions. Please note that TFP is not recommended for people with severe suicidal ideation and/or substance abuse or eating disorders.

Cognitive Behavior Therapy (CBT)

Cognitive Behavioral Therapy was developed by Dr. Aaron T. Beck, when he was a psychiatrist at the University of Pennsylvania. It's rooted in the premise that one's emotions, thoughts, physical sensations, and actions are linked. The idea that one's negative thoughts and feelings trap one in a vicious cycle is at its core. The primary goal of CBT is to break this cycle breaking problems into small chunks.

CBT is also very structured and focuses on current problems, not a client's past. It explores different ways to think to improve managing one's feelings. 'Homework' tasks are given as practice and assessed at next session (Matusiewicz et al., 2010). Full-cooperation and fidelity is expected and necessary for effectiveness.

CBT may be completed over shorter periods of time compared to other types of talk-therapies. It's offered in blocks ranging between six and twenty sessions. Sessions may be completed in individual, couple, and/or family sessions. However, this approach is not recommended for those with more complex mental health needs and/or learning difficulties.

Psychoanalytic Psychotherapy

Psychoanalytic psychotherapy is a talking therapy based on modern research derived from the theories of Sigmund Freud. It's centered around the premise that negative childhood experiences are repressed but continue to influence an individual's emotional stability as an adult. It focuses on emotions and how they are expressed, as well as why specific feelings and situations are avoided.

In sessions, the client and therapist delve into the past and discuss one's thoughts and feelings. Therapists guide their client to uncover hidden meanings, thought patterns, and behaviors that contribute to current struggles or issues (Paris, 2009). Keep in mind that because psychoanalytic therapy is personalized, the relationship between you and your therapist is critical to making notable progress as part of the treatment process.

Sessions are typically on a weekly or bi-weekly basis spanning over a minimum of a year, possibly longer depending on the client's needs. It may be done in individual or couple sessions. This approach has proven effectiveness for personality disorders, as well as obsessive-compulsive disorder, anxiety, depression, phobias, sexual issues, and many other mental health conditions.

Cognitive Analytical Therapy (CAT)

Cognitive Analytical Therapy (CAT) was developed by Dr. Anthony Ryle at Guy's and St. Thomas' Hospital in London. It's an individualized and structured therapy. It typically lasts about sixteen weeks, but on average it ranges between four and twenty-four weeks in duration. CAT's underlying premises are rooted in both object relations and social development theories.

CAT therapy analyzes past experiences in order to understand why a person has developed habitual patterns in the way they think, feel, and act. The therapist works with clients to map out problem patterns, physically charting connections on paper. While CAT has similarities to CBT, the main difference is that CAT does look back to the past to determine where particular challenges started. The ultimate goal of CAT is to facilitate the client in developing new ways of coping and methods to change negative thinking patterns (Kellett, et al., 2013).

In CAT therapy, a strong emphasis is placed upon the client's responses to others in their relationships, as opposed to problems occurring within the individual in isolation. Thus, those who struggle with interpersonal relationships would benefit from this type of therapy. This collaborative approach also has achieved success in those with personality disorders, anxiety, depression, phobias, eating disorders, and relationship issues.

Schema-Focused Therapy (SFT)

Schema- focused therapy was developed by Dr. Jeffery Young. This approach focuses on identifying and changing specific, unhealthy ways of thinking. The underlying theory of this approach presumes one's basic childhood needs–safety, acceptance, and need for love and affection–were inadequately met. Thus, an individual developed unhealthy ways of interpreting and interacting, which are called maladaptive–or unhealthy–schemas. (Schemas are thinking and behavior patterns that are connected to one's sense of self and their world).

During SFT sessions, therapists work with clients to identify and link their past events in their life to their current symptoms. This approach targets maladaptive schemas prevalent in those with BPD, such as those involving abandonment, emotional deprivation, and defectiveness.

Some of the therapeutic techniques utilized during schema therapy include using Gestalt-based imagery flash cards to create messages, a form of role play known as chair work, and writing about feelings and thoughts in a diary-style format. Its goal is to change destructive behavior patterns, foster building nurturing relationships, and to increase feelings of self-worth and adequacy. SFT has produced positive outcomes when utilized to treat personality disorders, posttraumatic stress, chronic depression, substance abuse, anxiety, as well as relationship issues (Young, et.al., 2003).

One consideration is that this form of treatment is lengthy, as it's commonly utilized in treating more complex and chronic mental disorders. Typically SFT is recommended for approximately two sessions per week over an average of three years. Thus, its more expensive and time consuming than other forms of therapy.

Mindfulness-Based Cognitive Therapy (MBCT)

Mindfulness-Based Cognitive Therapy (MBCT) is a modified form of cognitive therapy that incorporates mindfulness practices, such as meditation and breathing exercises. In many cases MBCT is coupled with other therapies, such as DBT or CBT. Its core philosophies are derived from the principles of Buddhist mediation, primarily in achieving awareness, tranquility, and insight.

MBCT is typically a group therapy, which usually meets once a week for a two-hour session lead by a trained professional over eight weeks. It focuses on managing one's emotions in the present. Rather than avoiding negative emotions, techniques, such as meditation and other mindfulness exercises help clients gain clarity by observing and identifying their feelings. The goal is to move away from automatic reactions and towards replacing negative thoughts with positive ones (Parra-Delgado & Latorre-Postigo, 2013). Homework assignments in which participants practice meditation techniques and listen to audio recordings for forty-five minutes a day, six days a week, are required.

  Empirical research on MBCT's effectiveness as a stand-alone therapy for BPD is limited. Yet, research has shown positive outcomes in using mindfulness practices to cope with stress and effectiveness in treating chronic depression. Clinical studies have shown that participating in MBCT may be linked to a reduction in amygdala activity (Ivanovski & Malhi, 2007). Practicing mindfulness meditation can be done in conjunction with other types of therapy and is often incorporated into therapeutic treatment plans.

Systems Training for Emotional Predictability and Problem Solving (STEPPS)

Systems Training for Emotional Predictability and Problem Solving (STEPPS) was developed by Nancee Blum. It's an evidence-based program that has shown effectiveness when used to supplement other forms of treatment for BPD. One of the main goals of STEPPS is to educate and de-stigmatize the diagnosis. The twenty-week program is taught in a group setting, in a seminar or classroom style format. Typically, it's led by two trainers and meets once a week for two hours.

STEPPS begins by helping participants understand that BPD stems from a biological vulnerability that meet with certain environmental factors. It addresses the emotional intensity of the disorder through teaching awareness, and emotional and behavior management skills. Trainers facilitate clients in learning to recognize and predict their emotional reactions. The main focus is to help them acquire and develop the coping skills taught.

The STEPPS program can facilitate improving interpersonal relationships as people in the borderline's life, such as family and friends, are included in the training. Loved ones are utilized as reinforcers of the coping skills taught. Those with self-harm issues or suicidal ideation are directed to their individual therapist or emergency mental health services. Thus, the STEPPS program tends to be recommended by therapists in addition to another form of treatment (Blum, et al., 2008).

Also, this program has a follow-up component called STAIRWAYS. This one-year follow-up group meets twice a month after the completion of STEPPS. STAIRWAYS is oriented towards relationship management, impulsivity control, and staying on track, or relapse prevention.

***

I hope this overview narrows and refines your search when you're googling mental health practices. Depending on where you live, the types of therapy available will vary. I suggest asking your physician and/or mental health provider for recommendations of practices that specialize in treating personality disorders or specific therapeutic approaches. You should always consult a licensed mental health professional when developing a treatment plan.

CHAPTER FOUR

Coping Strategies

This chapter describes a variety of coping strategies for the DSM-5 criteria explained in this volume. The first set of strategies applies to the person with BPD and the next chapter overviews strategies more geared towards a borderline's loved ones.

It's important to note that some strategies may feel awkward and ineffective, at first. You may need to practice using techniques several times before you notice results. If you feel increased anxiety or panicky while trying a new strategy, stop, and select another one to work on. If you're fortunate enough to have access to mental health services, I recommend discussing techniques and outcomes with your therapist.

Coping and Management Strategies

Seek Support, Don't Wait

I'm beginning with this one because many people with BPD believe they are burden to others. If you are experiencing passive suicidal ideation (wishing you were dead or thinking about dying, but with no concrete plans) or active suicidal ideation (not only thinking about suicide, but you have the intent and a plan), reach out for immediate support.

You can reach out to a person you trust, your therapist (if you have one) or a mental health professional, call a crisis hotline, contact the National Suicide Prevention Lifeline at 1-800-273-8255, or call 9-1-1. You may also go to the emergency room at your local hospital.

Through my experiences working at a crisis hotline and in a therapeutic group home for girls with behavioral and psychiatric issues, I have found that the quality and level of care varies immensely depending upon the professional(s) and/or volunteers staffing the above organizations. I cannot emphasize enough to keep trying others if one person or place is unresponsive.

Don't be afraid to contact emergency services in your area. Sometimes due to the unfortunate lack of access to health care (both mental and physical), this may be the best route to getting the immediate services you need. First responders and emergency service workers are trained to deal with suicide and have immediate access to mental health services, 24-7.

Listen To Music For Mood Regulation

When listening to music as a coping mechanism, your purpose(s) will vary. If you are listening for a diversion or as a distraction, the music doesn't need to match your current mood. Though if you are in need of solace and aim to feel less alone, the genre should reflect upon your current emotional state. You may use music as a discharge. For example, if you want to release anger, you can blast your favorite angsty songs and belt out the lyrics. This can provide an outlet for your frustration.

After trying this strategy, I suggest writing down or discussing how you felt and what you observed afterwards. If listening to soothing, classic tones, for instance, didn't relieve your anxiety, listening to music may not be effective for managing that emotion for you. Ultimately, you need to determine what suits your individual tastes and actually helps improve your mood(s).

Engage in a Physical Activity

This coping skill as referred to as behavioral activation. This strategy involves keeping you physically engaged. Therefore, the goal of what you select is to distract from a stressor, an emotion, or obsessing over a reaction. If you play a sport or enjoy working out traditional physical exercise would be a good choice for you. Other examples of engaging activities include talking a walk, deep cleaning your room or particular area of your home, lawn work, high-energy dancing, and/or a DYI project, such as refinishing and painting a piece of furniture.

A Timed Ride It Out

Most intense emotional reactions or overpowering urges to engage in harmful activities typically subside after approximately three to ten minutes. Set the timer on your phone- or if you happen to have an old-school egg timer- for ten minutes and practice riding out the emotion. After ten minutes, reflect and think about how you feel and then note whether you can observe a difference in the way you feel.

Personally, I felt like a shark out of water when attempting this strategy and still struggle with activities like meditation and yoga. Again, consider attempting this a few times before deciding whether it works for you. It may take time before you become comfortable if practicing relaxation techniques are new to you.

Random Acts of Kindness

Doing something nice or helping someone has shown in clinical studies to boost one's subjective well-being. Positive correlations exist between improving one's self-esteem and self-image and altruistic behaviors (Curry et. al., 2018). Even small acts can produce those warm tingly feelings; the acts of kindness don't need to be labor-intensive or time-consuming to be rewarding. You may shovel an elderly neighbor's walkway, surprise your child's teacher with their favorite latte- or a basket of Lysol wipes- or you may simply offer to carry groceries for someone struggling. It may sound silly, but small gestures of kindness have been shown to reduce emotional pain.

If after delivering a couple doses of kindness, you found it made you feel good, you may extend your altruism by volunteering. Giving your time and expressing the goodness of human nature on a regular basis is way to feel good about yourself and improve your self-esteem. Further, it provides opportunities for you connect with others. Select a place or cause that suits your nature. For example, if you love dogs, choose a shelter or an advocacy group for pets.

If you're like, Hey, I haven't worked on my sense of self and my favorite person just left, so I don't know what I like, then consider a homeless shelter, food pantry, or domestic violence agency. Those types of organizations usually are in need of volunteers- and they're typically ran by open-minded professionals so they won't be judgmental about mental illness. Though, please be mindful of how much time is manageable and don't overextend yourself. Most organizations are extremely grateful for volunteers, even ones who can only commit to a few hours a month.

Breathing Exercises

Breathing deeply is a tried-and-true, simple relaxation method. As a surge of anxiety usually accompanies splitting episodes, this method can be beneficial for helping you stay grounded, in the present.

First, choose a quiet place to sit or lie. Then, focus your attention on your breathing patterns. Inhale slowly and deeply through your nose. Concentrate on breathing evenly while exhaling slowly out through your mouth. Relax your jaw as you blow air out and purse your lips slightly. Watch your stomach rise and fall with each breath. It may even be helpful to place your hand on your stomach to feel each breath as you practice this exercise.

Repeat for several minutes until you start to feel calm. This technique should help prevent extreme feelings from taking over. Some people initially feel panicky or feel like these exercises aren't working. Please remember this type of breathing requires some practice and will become easier.

Progressive Muscle Relaxation (PMR)

If you feel the deep breathing described above isn't quite enough to relax you, you may find Progressive Muscle Relaxation (PMR) more helpful. You should be seated or laying down and in loose fitting clothing before beginning PMR.

First, as you inhale contract one muscle group, such as your buttocks, for five seconds to ten seconds. Then, exhale all at once (not gradually) while releasing the tension in that muscle group. Wait ten to twenty seconds before moving on to the next muscle group.

While releasing, focus on the changes you feel when each muscle group is relaxed. Close your eyes and visualize the stressful feelings floating out of your body. Gradually work your way up your body, repeating the contracting/relaxing of your isolated muscle groups.

There are a variety of modified versions of this technique, but most modern variations are based on Jacobson's original concept of systematically squeezing and releasing isolated muscle groups (Mackereth & Tomilson, 2010). Watching videos showing someone modeling PMR and practicing along with them may make this strategy easier to understand.

Therapeutic Journaling

Journaling is a way to channel negative thoughts, feelings, and reactions in a constructive way. When done with fidelity, this form of self-expression can lead to personal growth. Also, this strategy offers long-term benefits as it promotes self-reflection. In writing down your thoughts and feelings, you are forced to focus on details you may have otherwise missed. Through journaling you learn to listen to, rather than avoid, overwhelming or conflicted emotions (Thompson, 2010).

Your therapist may provide structured questions, topics, or open-ended sentence stems for journaling. Some common topics are mood tracking (writing down what happened before, during, and after shifts in your mood), listing triggers and reactions, and identifying which emotions have been most prominent over the past few days. Sentence starters may include, 'The thing I am most worried about are…' or 'I notice my mood swings when…happens…"

If you are actively participating in therapy specific prompts may be given as homework. Or you may decide to keep a journal, using your own prompts to better analyze your emotional reactions. For instance, you may write about conflicts in your interpersonal relationships. Some sample prompts or questions include, What was my initial response when the problem, incident, or splitting behavior(s) occurred? What happened leading up to the incident? What emotions did I display at the time? What were my thoughts at the time? What lessons can be learned?

A gratitude journal is another writing technique to facilitate you in changing negative thinking patterns. At the end of each day or week, write down people, actions, or events that you appreciate. Keep in mind you don't have to be super happy or perfectly content to be grateful. This could be a supplement to another type of journaling as well or other therapies.

Another form of journaling is letter writing. You write a letter to someone about issues, conflicts, or emotional reactions you are experiencing involving the targeted person. The letter usually is not actually mailed to the person. For example, you may might write a letter to a deceased parent to release lingering feelings.

Keeping a traditional diary style journal can be a positive way to avoid triple texting a partner, providing an outlet for your fluctuating feelings.

Express Yourself Through Art

For me, creative writing is an outlet for my negative emotions. It calms me down when I'm feeling anxious or having erratic mood swings. It's a solace when I need a distraction–especially from sending wicked long texts to someone I should probably stop messaging altogether.

Your form of expression may be anything from music to theatrical or visual arts to cooking or photography. If you haven't unlocked your artistic gift yet, I encourage to reflect upon what types of activities or art forms brought you joy as a child or teen. You may ask family members or friends if they remember a past talent you may have kicked to the wayside.

You also may want to research or make a list of any types of art that piques your interest. It may take a few weeks, but keep revisiting your search. Consider experimenting with a few and wade into your creative waters. Identifying and discovering a form of artistic expression that truly brings you joy can facilitate you in developing a stronger sense of self.

Connecting with Others

Scientific evidence supports that being socially connected is a core psychological need, essential for people to feel content with their lives. Further, clinical studies show that fostering these connections is critical to health and wellness (Hallowell, 1999). Having quality social support systems and feeling connected to others plays a significant role in maintaining one's mental and physical health, such as decreasing depressive symptoms, improved cardiovascular health, and higher cancer survival rates.

There is an abundance of research highlighting the link between maintaining positive social bonds and good overall health. Basically, the human brain is wired to socially connect. This is important for people with BPD because oxytocin- the bonding hormone- is released during social interactions with others. (Gordon, et.al., 2013). Oxytocin works with other neurotransmitters which increase feelings of happiness, enhance one's mood, and decrease feelings of loneliness and depression.

As you are aware, borderlines initial interactions with people can be phenomenal- especially when this new friend quickly becomes your favorite person- but maintaining friendships is a rocky road. Social distancing has recently presented more obstacles with expanding your social circle. As everyone is still navigating uncertain times, you may need to revisit some of the suggestions in our everchanging world. I will leave out online dating apps for obvious reasons, though, I have known a few people that have had luck on the Bumble BFF in making platonic friends.

One way that offers the dual purpose of connecting and honing in on your creative passions is to enroll in a class that intrigues you. This could be anything from academic courses to pottery or culinary classes. Seeking out meet-ups in your area organized by a theme or activity such as hiking, surfing, gardening, or book clubs is another way to grow connections as well as prevent you from staying in toxic interpersonal relationships. Volunteering, to reiterate, is a positive way to not only give back, but it lends itself to building bonds and authentic friendships–those quality ones we all want– with people in your community.

Interacting with others face-to-face has other benefits, such as deterring loneliness and the tendency to isolate. Also, curating your own interests and developing a more diverse circle of friends facilitates you in not becoming overly attached to one person. It's a healthy distraction, giving you meaningful ways to spend your time and allowing you to reap the benefits of truly feeling connected to other people.

Support Groups Participation (In-Person or Online)

Participating in BPD support groups is a way to connect with others who understand your perspective. Finding a borderline personality disorder group that meets face-to-face has been a challenge for me. Availability will be dependent upon on where you physically live.

I have participated in several online support groups, some have been more helpful than others. While it's healthy to vent and release your frustrations, please keep in mind that if the majority of the group's posts tend to be negative, you may want to try another group. Bottom line, you need to feel like you're connecting as well as giving and receiving positive feedback. After interacting, you should feel a sense of not being alone and, in general, better about yourself.

Practice Open Communication

This coping strategy differs from the first one listed in that it refers to talking to loved ones about your BPD symptoms, in non-crisis situations. I hope this book (and subsequent volumes) will be a useful tool in explaining the complexities of the disorder. It's best to sit down and read sections of this book with your loved one when both parties are calm and there's no current conflict on the brink.

It's important that your loved one is open-minded and shows a willingness to learn more about BPD. Please beware of those who try to convince you that mental illnesses aren't 'real' or of gaslighting techniques. (Gaslighting is a form of persistent manipulation that causes someone to doubt themselves, and their own sense of perception and self-worth). For instance, if a person causes you to question your sanity or accuses you of being too sensitive, this should be a red-flag. Also, if you spend a lot of time apologizing, doubting your feelings or judgements, or worry that you are inadequate based on how this person interacts with you, you need to talk to a trained mental health professional about the situation and further explore research on gaslighting tactics.

Making communication a priority and identifying ways to improve it is the first step. However, it can't be one-sided. In order for your efforts to be worthwhile, it needs to be with a person who's respectful and willing to put in genuine effort. If you have mental health coverage, participating in couples or family therapy is another excellent way to enhance communication skills. Additionally, working together on the workbook pages in the last chapter can facilitate meaningful conversations about how BPD impacts your thinking and reactions and about coping strategies that can help you manage symptoms.

Maintaining Healthy Habits (i.e. sleeping, eating, exercise)

I used to sigh whenever my doctor or therapist asked questions about my eating, sleeping, or exercising habits. I realize now they should not be overlooked or ignored. These seemingly simple daily patterns have a profound impact on your physical and mental health. I encourage you to speak with your physician about what is best for you and how to make changes if your current patterns are not conducive with balancing your physical and mental health.

Dissociation Specific Coping Strategies

The strategies described below may be more helpful for depersonalization and derealization, although some may be used to manage other symptoms as well. Most of the copying strategies focus on grounding yourself in the present by focusing on sensory experiences.

Activate Your Taste Buds

Chewing on a minty gum or sucking your favorite flavor of a hard candy can help bring you back into the present. Slowly eat something with an intense flavor, such as salt-and-vinegar chips or one of your favorite snacks. If you want to calm down, try something soothing such as hot tea or your favorite soup.

Using Aromatic Scents

Smelling certain spices or aromas may help ground you. You may want to use essential oils, diffusers, or a type of aromatherapy to snap you out of a dissociative state. Light a fragrant candle, smell flowers, or spritz your favorite perfume. You may you respond best to stronger fragrances, such as citrusy or floral scents.

Using Touch

If you're not feeling enough, holding ice cubes or running your hands under water can help redirect your dissociation. Some people may prefer warmth, such as from a heating pad or electric blanket. You may also grip a textured object, such as a stress balls, or try snuggling under a fuzzy blanket or cuddling with a pet. Again, it's about discovering what works best for you.

Listening to Sound

Listening to your favorite music, ringing a bell, or blowing a whistle may jolt you out of your dissociative state. Also, you may listen to nature or ocean sounds on a sound machine or an ambient sound app.

Using Sight

Focusing on an image that captures your attention may draw you back from a dissociative state. You could use an object in your immediate environment, such as a vivid painting, your favorite photo, or count all of the pieces of furniture around you. Concentrating on a puzzle or completing a word search or sudoku puzzle are other grounding techniques that may help you connect with the here and now.

Warm Bath/Shower

When I was at the behavioral health hospital, I could totally relate as another patient shared her thoughts on this coping strategy, I'm bouncing off the walls, and my therapist tells me to take a bubble bath! For most symptoms with BPD, this isn't enough. However, I figured I would include it as it may work for some. Try to lose yourself in the sensations of the warm water or the smell of the soap. Allow the sensations to distract you from the situation by focusing on relaxing your muscles.

Develop a Plan Ahead of Time

Being prepared for depersonalization and/or derealization by having a plan and objects in place is helpful. Share this plan with a loved one and discuss what you need them to do if you dissociate. Keeping flavored, scented, or other sensory items in a special box, so that they're easy to locate when the need arises may be beneficial.

***

By no means is this list of coping strategies exhaustive, yet it should provide a good place to start exploring what works to help manage your BPD symptoms. I encourage you to flip back and review this chapter when completing the workbook pages as you decide which management techniques you feel comfortable testing out.

CHAPTER FIVE

Coping Strategies and Communication Techniques

This chapter focuses on strategies and communication techniques for the loved one(s) of a person with BPD. I encourage you to discuss the strategies within the context of your interpersonal relationship. Elaborate upon what you both envision implementing the chosen strategies looking like in your daily lives. Give specific, real-world examples of actions each person would take, as applied to your circumstances. Be as detailed as possible when deciding when certain behaviors will occur, what each person may do or say, and how often the strategy is expected to be carried out.

Keep in mind there may be techniques not listed that help enhance understanding for your relationship. If either person has other strategies they would like to try, have a conversation about how you think they would be helpful. The purpose of selecting coping strategies is for them to be practical, meaningful, and effective.

Educate Yourself

Reading books and journal articles on borderline personality disorder will enable you better understand your loved one with BPD. Reliable literature and videos can illustrate why a borderline's emotions are so difficult to regulate. BPD can be a confusing diagnosis. Please do not expect to grasp BPD in one sitting. It will take time to digest the complicated and often conflicting criteria.

There are many misconceptions about what people with BPD experience and too many demeaning stereotypes to count. Educating yourself about why the fear of abandonment and emotional dysregulation are driving forces is essential to fully comprehending the disorder. As you begin to comprehend the interconnectedness of the symptoms, your connection with your loved one will strengthen. Deepening your knowledge on how a borderline's thought patterns impact their emotional reactions will give you a clearer understanding of how to best support your loved one.

Practice Validation

Validation is acknowledging someone's feelings, thoughts, perceptions, and beliefs. It's not about agreeing with them, it's about making an attempt to understand how they are feeling. Dismissing or ignoring a borderlines emotions is not only excruciatingly painful, it's counterproductive in maintaining fruitful communication and in building trust. Validation is to fulfilling and lasting relationships what carbon is to living things–essential. Without this essential skill, stable bonds are unable to be formed and the relationship will often fail.

To develop your validation skills, start by paying attention to what your loved one says by actively listening. Make eye contact and concentrate without any extraneous distractions. After processing their words, instead of saying, *Stop being so dramatic* or *you're overreacting*, you should acknowledge their feelings with statements like, *I can tell you're hurting, it's got to be awful to feel that way*. Being conscious of your word choice as it sets the tone. Empathetic comments like, *I am on your side, Thank you for sharing this with me, I can see how hard you're working. It must be difficult to be in this situation,* or *Let me make sure I've got things straight, you feel like you don't matter when this happens.*

After you've given them a chance to share, ask open-ended questions to find out more about their problem, situation, and/or point-of-view. Asking what happened, instead of what's wrong, shows you're concerned. Try using statements like, *Tell me more about…, I believe in you, I'm sorry I hurt you,* or *Can you explain more about why you're thinking this?* This type of phrasing helps you gain insight and shows that you care. Put your own voice into the dialogue and be specific to the context. It's important your concern and words are genuine. With practice, validation will become more natural to execute and will clear up minor misunderstandings before they escalate into explosive arguments.

Validating your loved one's feelings communicates that they matter to you. Listening with empathy enables you to see situations from their point-of-view. You don't have to fix your partner's problem or agree with them. Rather you should acknowledge and identify with what they are feeling. Imagine a loved one was diagnosed with a rare muscle condition–one you didn't know much about. To better understand their condition, you'd ask questions in a respectful, compassionate way to make sense out of what they are thinking, feeling, and experiencing.

However, when a person doesn't feel like their partner is listening, cares, or is rejecting them, communication breaks down. Walls are thrown up and nine times out of ten those walls were constructed out of the stones of invalidation. After repeated invalidating responses, such as being ignored, judged, or having your feelings labeled as wrong, people tend to shut down, growing resentful. Most borderlines have a higher-than-average need for acknowledgment and attentiveness due to their heightened sensitivity to rejection. They require a little extra affirmation from their partners.

Seeking healthy validation is not unique to BPD. I've perused an overwhelming number of blog posts, articles, and studies that have attributed having an invalidating partner as a key factor in relationship failure and divorce. However, on the contrary, I've also discovered an over-abundance of articles and posts online warning borderlines to stop seeking validation.

I used to feel ashamed for needing–and sometimes craving–affirmation in my relationships. Yet, I realized that I desire to be in a relationship where my partner acknowledges my thoughts and empathizes with my feelings. I've learned that there is nothing wrong with communicating my needs and expectations for emotional validation. If my partner doesn't truly want to devout time to sharing our inner most thoughts and strengthening our intimate connections, then there is no point in even being together.

When someone pays attention (i.e. looks at you, not their phone) to what you say and makes a genuine effort to understand, you feel accepted and less vulnerable. The need for affection, love, companionship, and acceptance can be met through interactions with family, friends, and romantic partners. According to Maslow's Hierarchy of Needs, the social need for love and belongingness is inherent to human nature and motivation. (Maslow, 1971). Wanting validation is not a negative quality, it's essential for relationships to thrive.

Be Responsive

When your borderline is trying to contact you, it's helpful to be as responsive as possible. If you don't respond, they feel rejected or worry you're about to leave them (back to that hyperactive amygdala). Borderlines internalize the lack of a response. They feel like they did something wrong, like they aren't good enough, or that you hate them. As more time passes their internal fears become increasingly difficult to control. Eventually that fear of abandonment seizes them and they believe, in the moment, that you're leaving them.

Having an honest conversation about responding to text messages, calls, and/or email is important for your relationship to thrive. Given varying family dynamics, schedules, and work obligations, both people need to voice their expectations and reach an agreement on how responding will be handled.

For example, if you know you'll be in meeting at work and unable to use your phone, communicate why you will be unavailable ahead of time with your partner. If you are a person who needs 'time alone to process' after an argument, you and your partner need to agree upon for how much post-argument alone time is acceptable. Avoiding a person with BPD will escalate any disagreement ten-fold. The emotional duress that unresponsiveness causes the borderline is equivalent to holding your hand to the burner on a stove.

With the emotional dysregulation, this can lead to self-hatred and often destructive and/or self-harm behaviors. It's difficult for a person with BPD to handle perceived rejection (or actual rejection) because they blame themselves, especially after an argument or disagreement. Even if the borderline is making progress, the added stress of a quarrel will make emotions and fears more difficult to manage.

Recognize, Understand, and Avoid Triggers

Recognizing and discussing situations that elicit a borderlines fear of rejection or abandonment is an effective way to prevent arguments. Have a conversation about specific triggers that occur and what both people can do to prevent pulling the trigger. Being aware of which behaviors or situations tend to cause intense emotional reactions in your life can make a difference.

Once particular triggers are acknowledged and discussed, simple steps can be taken to avoid some of them altogether.

Show Your Appreciation

People with BPD often go above and beyond to do special things for their loved one, especially romantic partners or favorite people. They have a strong desire to make you happy. They crave receiving that same show of love and affirmation in return. If they don't receive it, borderlines are more prone to quickly begin feeling unloved and taken for granted. Like most, people with BPD want sincere validation and genuine love. Appreciating someone makes them feel good about what they do, feel better about themselves, and thus, strengthens a relationship.

The lack of appreciation often leads to complacency, resentment, and eventual break-ups with many couples, even without the presence of BPD. Communicate your expectations and tell your partner when you do not feel appreciated. If you wait too long or stay silent, your frustration will escalate and then it's only a matter of time before the emotional connection starts to wither.

In my experience, once the intimate bond is weakened, it's not likely to regain its original strength. I have been in a few relationships where I repeatedly expressed how I no longer felt appreciated and I was not receiving what I needed and deserved. However, by the time they came around and started showering me with attention, gifts, and romantic gestures, it was too late. After feeling neglected and empty for too long, I was no longer interested or in love.

There are many ways to show appreciation. Thank your loved one for the little things they do every day, like cooking for you or doing your laundry. Acknowledge specific traits you love about your partner. Surprise your partner with a romantic note or card. Show affection and make time to spend time together doing things you enjoy as well as for physical intimacy.

Giving gifts is another way that makes someone feel special. When you love someone, you should *want* to be generous, as it reminds your loved one how much you cherish them. The gifts don't need to be expensive, just thoughtful.

Show love even when you are tired or don't feel like it. Giving sincere praise and compliments is another way to make your partner feel loved and valued. Both partners should make an effort to be one another's biggest motivator and cheerleader, offering encouragement and (sometimes) making sacrifices to support each other.

Provide Reassurance

While someone with BPD needs reassurance in different types of interpersonal relationships, it's critical in romantic ones. When the borderline in your life needs reassurance you should assume that their default is either, *You don't care about me,* or *You're going to leave me.* Even if you don't fully comprehend why your partner is feeling insecure or fearful in the moment, acknowledge their feelings and provide validation-based support. Ask them why they feel a certain way, actively listen, and then provide the assurance based on what they explained to you. Avoid going on the defensive with a response such as, *I don't know how you got I don't care about you from that….* They wouldn't be seeking the affirmation if they didn't value you and your opinion.

Give specific examples to show that your loved one with BPD matters to you. Comfort them by reminding of things you do that express how much you care, such as *I always call you on your lunch break because I want to know how your day's going and hear your voice because I care about you*, or *we've been together for three years and they've been the three greatest years because I love you*. You should provide extra reassurance, even after they seem satisfied. This reinforces that it's okay to talk about their feelings and that they are not a burden.

Have an open and in-depth conversation about reassurance to figure out what triggers self-doubt and what worries them the most. No one's a mind reader, so communication is essential when it comes to what kind and how much reassurance is needed. Work together to determine specific ways that you can soothe their doubts. You may decide to write down a few concrete examples on the workbook pages in the next chapter.

You're not doing anything wrong. It's not that your loved one with BPD didn't believe you when you told them only yesterday how deeply you care about them. It's just the opposite. *Your* reassurance matters to them because they care about you so intensely. If they didn't find comfort and security in your approval, they wouldn't fight so vehemently for it.

Accept Setbacks

Regardless of where your loved one is in terms of therapy or in managing their symptoms, learn to accept set-backs. For instance, you probably wouldn't blame a person who received a heart valve replacement for experiencing difficulties with the valve eighteen months later. It's important to take into account that stressful life situations can prompt setbacks in progress, such as frustrations at work, the death of a loved one, abrupt shifts in schedules, or changes in routines.

Remind your loved one that it's not their fault. Placing blame or criticism will only perpetuate negative thinking patterns. Your encouragement and positive mindset will encourage them to remain hopeful. Your attitude can be influential in alleviating guilt that frequently occurs when a borderline back slides with using coping strategies. Be mindful that coping with and treating BPD, is about progress and persistence not perfection.

Seek Support from Mental Health Professionals

Participating in individual, couples, or family therapy will facilitate you in supporting your borderline. Putting in the time and extra effort reiterates that they are important to you and that you value them. Also, if you and your partner struggle with communication or using coping strategies, couples therapy is an excellent way to develop and practice these important techniques.

If you have anxiety about helping your loved one manage their BPD symptoms or believe it's causing you emotional duress, a mental health professional can facilitate you in setting appropriate boundaries. In order to build trust and offer support, you need to stay balanced and take care of your needs as well.

***

The coping strategies overviewed in this chapter are not the only ones that may work in supporting your loved one with BPD. Particular techniques, such as validation and reassurance, are integral in developing effective communication skills necessary to sustain a healthy relationship. You should revisit this chapter when completing the workbook pages and selecting strategies to support your partner and strengthen your relationship.

CHAPTER SIX

Improving Interpersonal Relationships Worksheets

I believe people with BPD are capable of having fulfilling and lasting relationships, both romantic and platonic. It's unfortunate that negative media portrayal and unreliable sources online perpetuate the stigma that borderlines can't have healthy, long-term relationships. Many of these stereotypes tend to focus on romantic relationships. After searching relentlessly for evidence-based statistics, I couldn't locate any scientific data to support this myth. However, I did discover that divorce percentages amongst marriages in which one spouse has BPD compared to overall divorce rates in the US show no statistical significance. Also, a longitudinal research study found that BPD symptoms did not predict ten-year divorce rates (Lavner et al., 2015).

Open communication and validation are essential to any happy, thriving relationship. Discuss your different communication styles as you identify the coping strategies you agree to work on together. Some people prefer to talk more, some like affectionate touches, while others respond better to non-verbal cues and facial expressions. Share and explain your thoughts, preferences, fears, and expectations. Be cognizant that with a little patience from loved ones, people with BPD can make dedicated, loyal friends and passionate, loving partners.

I disagree with cliché advice, *You need to work on yourself before you can be in a relationship.* I think this idea perpetuates the stigma of mental illness, as no one would give that advice to some with a physical condition, like diabetes. I can't imagine someone saying, *Well, until she gets her insulin levels under control, she just needs to focus on herself.* I believe a borderline can be in a romantic relationship while struggling with symptoms and/or participating in treatment. I feel that with the *right* partner–one who is accepting, loyal, and willing to learn about BPD–the relationship can be supportive, rewarding, and flourish.

As referred to earlier in the book, relevant psychology research supports that fostering close relationships and human interaction has positive effects on one's mental well-being. Spending time with a partner as well as quality friends leads to significantly less time spent isolating and experiencing loneliness. More time spent connecting and bonding with others has been proven to decrease the occurrence and severity of comorbidities, such as depression, anxiety, and suicidal ideation.

As you fill in the workbook pages, I encourage you to refer back to the symptoms, your notes, and re-read the strategies, as needed. Two sample worksheets are included. The first is completed by a borderline, utilizing coping strategies to improve their interpersonal relationship(s), on their own. The second sample is filled out by a person with BPD and their loved one. In both, three emotional reactions and coping strategies are listed. However, selecting one or two, to start, is more realistic and manageable. Begin with small steps, as it's quality, not quantity that counts.

At the bottom of each worksheet, there is a *Check Progress* section. Evaluate your progress every one to two weeks. It's okay to carry some of the same goals over to subsequent workbook pages. Please keep in mind that finding what coping strategies work for you is a work in progress.

Date: 9/1

Sample:
Person with BPD Completing Worksheet To Improve Friendship With Favorite Person

Reactions/Triggers/Behaviors Causing Conflicts in My Relationship:

1.	I split on my favorite person (FP) when she changes plans. I rage, yell at her, and don't speak to her for days.
2.	I isolate myself if my FP has plans with other friends when I ask her to hang out or make plans with me.
3.	I dissociate during or after arguments/disagreements with my FP.

Coping Strategies (Borderline):

1.	Instead of splitting & yelling at her if she has to change plans, I will engage in a physical activity. I will swim laps in the pool or work out on the elliptical.
2.	I cope with isolating when my FP has other plans by enrolling in a pottery class downtown and connecting with new people there.
3.	I will try activating my taste buds by keeping peppermint Altoids in my handbag.

Coping Strategies (Loved One):

1. *blank if completing on your own
2.
3.

Progress Check   Date: 9/8

What I/we think worked well:

The physical activity –swimming– worked well when she couldn't go for Sushi will me on Tuesday. I swam for 45 minutes before replying to her text and had calmed down by the time I finished swimming.

What I/we think needs improvement or changes:

I think using peppermints is not strong enough to help my dissociation. I will choose another strategy in addition. Also, I need to improve my motivation to connect with others. I will enroll in the pottery class this week.

Date: 9/3

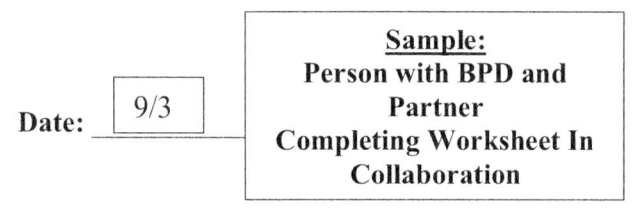

**Sample:
Person with BPD and Partner Completing Worksheet In Collaboration**

Reactions/Triggers/Behaviors
Causing Conflicts in My Relationship:

1.	When my partner doesn't respond quickly to my texts, I become angry, lash out, and triple text him.
2.	I cry, get upset, and start an argument with my partner when he tells me I'm overreacting.
3.	I worry that my partner's getting sick of me and will leave me. I react by texting too much and repeatedly asking him to tell me he's not and that he loves me. I split on him by saying he's not romantic after he gets annoyed and says he must not be enough for me.

Coping Strategies (Borderline):

1.	I will try open communication and talk to my partner about this. When he's unavailable at work, I will try listening to music to calm my mood and regulate emotions.
2.	I will cope by using 'a timed ride it out' and set my timer for 10 minutes. I will practice validation, both ways, with my partner and ask my therapist for help with this skill.
3.	When I doubt my partners feelings or think he's leaving me, I will try therapeutic journaling to get my feelings out. I will also try open communication about my need for more reassurance.

Coping Strategies (Loved One):

1.	I will make a point of being more responsive and return messages as soon as possible. I will send **1** 'thinking of you' text each day and let her know when work will be too busy to text.
2.	I will look up examples of validation. I will print to use when listening, questioning, and responding when my partner is trying to explain something that happened.
3.	I will talk with my partner and give her verbal reassurance that I'm not leaving at least 3 times per week. When she asks for reassurance I will give it and then give extra. I will leave her a note or card and do something special at least one week to be romantic.

Progress Check   **Date:**

What I/we think worked well:

We agree being more responsive worked on 4 out of 5 days. We're using the validation example language when discussing problems and issues. We're arguing less, so we will continue to practice this skill. The notes to each other have been wonderful and helped us reconnect.

What I/we think needs improvement or changes:

We need to continue working on being responsive and keep improving, but going in right direction. For the next workbook page, we need to be more specific on reassurance and work on asking for and giving it more often, even when our schedules become hectic.

Date:

**Reactions/Triggers/Behaviors
Causing Conflicts in My Relationship:**

1.
2.
3.

Coping Strategies (Borderline):

1.
2.
3.

Coping Strategies (Loved One):

1.
2.
3.

Progress Check   Date:

What I/we think worked well:
What I/we think needs improvement or changes:

Date:

**Reactions/Triggers/Behaviors
Causing Conflicts in My Relationship:**

1.
2.
3.

Coping Strategies (Borderline):

1.
2.
3.

Coping Strategies (Loved One):

1.
2.
3.

Progress Check   **Date:**

What I/we think worked well:
What I/we think needs improvement or changes:

Date:

Reactions/Triggers/Behaviors
Causing Conflicts in My Relationship:

1.
2.
3.

Coping Strategies (Borderline):

1.
2.
3.

Coping Strategies (Loved One):

1.
2.
3.

Progress Check   **Date:**

What I/we think worked well:
What I/we think needs improvement or changes:

Date:

**Reactions/Triggers/Behaviors
Causing Conflicts in My Relationship:**

1.
2.
3.

Coping Strategies (Borderline):

1.
2.
3.

Coping Strategies (Loved One):

1.
2.
3.

Progress Check   Date:

What I/we think worked well:
What I/we think needs improvement or changes:

Date:

**Reactions/Triggers/Behaviors
Causing Conflicts in My Relationship:**

1.
2.
3.

Coping Strategies (Borderline):

1.
2.
3.

Coping Strategies (Loved One):

1.

2.

3.

Progress Check   Date:

What I/we think worked well:
What I/we think needs improvement or changes:

Date:

**Reactions/Triggers/Behaviors
Causing Conflicts in My Relationship:**

1.
2.
3.

Coping Strategies (Borderline):

1.
2.
3.

Coping Strategies (Loved One):

1.

2.

3.

Progress Check   Date:

What I/we think worked well:

What I/we think needs improvement or changes:

Date:

**Reactions/Triggers/Behaviors
Causing Conflicts in My Relationship:**

1.
2.
3.

Coping Strategies (Borderline):

1.
2.
3.

Coping Strategies (Loved One):

1.
2.
3.

Progress Check   Date:

What I/we think worked well:
What I/we think needs improvement or changes:

Date:

**Reactions/Triggers/Behaviors
Causing Conflicts in My Relationship:**

1.
2.
3.

Coping Strategies (Borderline):

1.
2.
3.

Coping Strategies (Loved One):

1.
2.
3.

Progress Check   Date:

What I/we think worked well:
What I/we think needs improvement or changes:

Date:

**Reactions/Triggers/Behaviors
Causing Conflicts in My Relationship:**

1.
2.
3.

Coping Strategies (Borderline):

1.
2.
3.

Coping Strategies (Loved One):

1.

2.

3.

Progress Check   Date:

What I/we think worked well:
What I/we think needs improvement or changes:

Date:

**Reactions/Triggers/Behaviors
Causing Conflicts in My Relationship:**

1.
2.
3.

Coping Strategies (Borderline):

1.
2.
3.

Coping Strategies (Loved One):

1.
2.
3.

Progress Check   Date:

What I/we think worked well:
What I/we think needs improvement or changes:

Date:

**Reactions/Triggers/Behaviors
Causing Conflicts in My Relationship:**

1.
2.
3.

Coping Strategies (Borderline):

1.
2.
3.

Coping Strategies (Loved One):

1.

2.

3.

Progress Check   Date:

What I/we think worked well:
What I/we think needs improvement or changes:

Date:

**Reactions/Triggers/Behaviors
Causing Conflicts in My Relationship:**

1.
2.
3.

Coping Strategies (Borderline):

1.
2.
3.

Coping Strategies (Loved One):

1.
2.
3.

Progress Check   Date:

What I/we think worked well:
What I/we think needs improvement or changes:

Conclusion

The hard part is over! Criteria A of the DSM-5 is the most complex and overarching component as well as the cornerstone of BPD. Grasping the core features of emotional dysregulation and impairments with self and interpersonal functioning are key to understanding the other symptoms. I hope your understanding of the first criteria of your borderline personality disorder diagnosis is now much clearer.

I encourage you to re-read and to continue drawing connections from the examples given in this book to experiences in your own life. Processing the subpoints of criteria A will take time and reflection. This is the reason I have divided this series into separate, easier-to-digest volumes.

After wrapping your brain around the foundational core of BPD, you and your loved ones will be better equipped to comprehend how the emotional hypersensitivity, fear of abandonment, and your self-image impacts the other symptoms. The subsequent volumes of this series will expand upon the interconnectedness and explain B, C, D, and E of the DSM-5 criteria for BPD.

My aim in writing this series–for borderlines, by a borderline–is to unmask the enigmatic nature of BPD, eliminating misconceptions. I believe knowledge and communication will destigmatize the myths surrounding people with BPD and their relationships. I hope you walk away empowered and that your interpersonal relationships blossom.

If you found this book influential, enlightening, or refreshingly different, please write a review and share your thoughts.

XOXO

Alexis

About the Author

Alexis Sands attended the State University of New York at Potsdam and the University of North Carolina at Wilmington. She graduated with degrees in psychology and education, respectively. When she's not writing, she loves soaking in the sun at the beach, with a page-turner, cooking, paddle boarding, and spending time with her son.

Alexis is passionate about erasing the stigma associated with borderline personality disorder. She is also the author of *Slated: Blurred Borders Series, Book One* and *Split: Blurred Borders Series, Book Two*.

To Learn more about Alexis Sands, visit her at:

https://www.alexissands.com

Twitter: @AlexisSands6

Instagram: @AlexisSands6

REFERENCES

American Psychiatric Association. (2013). Diagnostic and statistical manual of mental disorders. (5th ed.). Arlington, VA: American Psychiatric Association

Bateman, A., & Fonagy, P. (2008). 8-year follow-up of patients treated for borderline personality disorder: mentalization-based treatment versus treatment as usual. The American journal of psychiatry, 165(5), 631–638.
https://doi.org/10.1176/appi.ajp.2007.07040636

Black, D. W., Pfohl, B., Blum, N., McCormick, B., Allen, J., North, C. S., et al. (2011). Attitudes toward borderline personality disorder: A survey of 706 mental health clinicians. CNS Spectrums, 16, 67–74

Blum, N., St John, D., Pfohl, B., Stuart, S., McCormick, B., Allen, J., Arndt, S., & Black, D. W. (2008). Systems Training for Emotional Predictability and Problem Solving (STEPPS) for outpatients with borderline personality disorder: a randomized controlled trial and 1-year follow-up. The American journal of psychiatry, 165(4), 468–478. https://doi.org/10.1176/appi.ajp.2007.07071079

Bourvis, N., Aouidad, A., Cabelguen, C., Cohen, D., & Xavier, J. (2017). How Do Stress Exposure and Stress Regulation Relate to Borderline Personality Disorder?. Frontiers in psychology, 8, 2054.
https://doi.org/10.3389/fpsyg.2017.02054

Brambilla, P., Soloff, P. H., Sala, M., Nicoletti, M. A., Keshavan, M. S., & Soares, J. C. (2004). Anatomical MRI study of borderline personality disorder patients. Psychiatry research, 131(2), 125–133.

Butler, E. A., Egloff, B., Wilhelm, F. H., Smith, N. C., Erickson, E. A., & Gross, J. J. (2003). The social consequences of expressive suppression. Emotion (Washington, D.C.), 3(1), 48–67.
https://doi.org/10.1037/1528-3542.3.1.48

Camilleri, V. A. (2007). Moderating factors. In V. A. Camilleri (Ed.), Healing the inner city child: Creative arts therapies with at-risk youth, (p. 50–56). Jessica Kingsley Publishers.

Chapman A. L. (2006). Dialectical behavior therapy: current indications and unique elements. Psychiatry (Edgmont (Pa. : Township)), 3(9), 62–68.

Crowell, S. E., Beauchaine, T. P., & Linehan, M. M. (2009). A biosocial developmental model of borderline personality: Elaborating and extending Linehan's theory. Psychological bulletin, 135(3), 495–510.

Curry, O. S., Rowland, L. A., Van Lissa, C. J., Zlotowitz, S., McAlaney, J., & Whitehouse, H. (2018). Happy to help? A systematic review and meta-analysis of the effects of performing acts of kindness on the well-being of the actor. Journal of Experimental Social Psychology, 76, 320–329.

Dabrowski, K. (1967). Personality-shaping through positive disintegration. Boston: Little, Brown.

Dinsdale, N., & Crespi, B. J. (2013). The borderline empathy paradox: evidence and conceptual models for empathic enhancements in borderline personality disorder. Journal of personality disorders, 27(2), 172–195.

Donegan, N. H., Sanislow, C. A., Blumberg, H. P., Fulbright, R. K., Lacadie, C., Skudlarski, P., Gore, J. C., Olson, I. R., McGlashan, T. H., & Wexler, B. E. (2003). Amygdala hyperreactivity in borderline personality disorder: implications for emotional dysregulation. Biological psychiatry, 54(11), 1284–1293. https://doi.org/10.1016/s0006-3223(03)00636-x

Farrell, J. M., Shaw, I. A., & Webber, M. A. (2009). A schema-focused approach to group psychotherapy for outpatients with borderline personality disorder: a randomized controlled trial. Journal of behavior therapy and experimental psychiatry, 40(2), 317–328. https://doi.org/10.1016/j.jbtep.2009.01.002

Faraone, S. V., Biederman, J., Spencer, T., Wilens, T., Seidman, L. J., Mick, E., & Doyle, A. E. (2000). Attention-deficit/hyperactivity disorder in adults: An overview. Biological Psychiatry, 48(1), 9–20.

Fonagy P. (2000). Attachment and borderline personality disorder. Journal of the American Psychoanalytic Association, 48(4), 1129–1187. https://doi.org/10.1177/00030651000480004070

Giesen-Bloo, J., van Dyck, R., Spinhoven, P., van Tilburg, W., Dirksen, C., van Asselt, T., Kremers, I., Nadort, M., & Arntz, A. (2006). Outpatient psychotherapy for borderline personality disorder: randomized trial of schema-focused therapy vs transference-focused psychotherapy. Archives of general psychiatry, 63(6), 649–658.

Gordon, I., Vander Wyk, B. C., Bennett, R. H., Cordeaux, C., Lucas, M. V., Eilbott, J. A., Zagoory-Sharon, O., Leckman, J. F., Feldman, R., & Pelphrey, K. A. (2013). Oxytocin enhances brain function in children with autism. Proceedings of the National Academy of Sciences of the United States of America, 110(52), 20953–20958. https://doi.org/10.1073/pnas.1312857110

Gross, J. J., John, O. P. (2003). Individual differences in two emotion regulation processes: Implications for affect, relationships, and well-being. Journal of Personality and Social Psychology, 85, 348–362.

Guitart-Masip, M., Pascual, J. C., Carmona, S., Hoekzema, E., Bergé, D., Pérez, V., Soler, J., Soliva, J. C., Rovira, M., Bulbena, A., & Vilarroya, O. (2009). Neural correlates of impaired emotional discrimination in borderline personality disorder: an fMRI study. Progress in neuro-psychopharmacology & biological psychiatry, 33(8), 1537–1545. https://doi.org/10.1016/j.pnpbp.2009.08.022

Herpertz, S. C., Dietrich, T. M., Wenning, B., Krings, T., Erberich, S. G., Willmes, K., Thron, A., & Sass, H. (2001). Evidence of abnormal amygdala functioning in borderline personality disorder: a functional MRI study. Biological psychiatry, 50(4), 292–298. https://doi.org/10.1016/s0006-3223(01)01075-7

Ivanovski, B., & Malhi, G. S. (2007). The psychological and neurophysiological concomitants of mindfulness forms of meditation. Acta neuropsychiatrica, 19(2), 76–91. https://doi.org/10.1111/j.1601-5215.2007.00175.x

Jackson, P. & Moyle, Vicky & Piechowski, Michael. (2009). Emotional Life and Psychotherapy of the Gifted in Light of Dabrowski's Theory. 10.1007/978-1-4020-6162-2_20.

Kellett, S., Bennett, D., Ryle, T., & Thake, A. (2013). Cognitive analytic therapy for borderline personality disorder: therapist competence and therapeutic effectiveness in routine practice. Clinical psychology & psychotherapy, 20(3), 216–225. https://doi.org/10.1002/cpp.796

Koenigsberg H. W. (2010). Affective instability: toward an integration of neuroscience and psychological perspectives. Journal of personality disorders, 24(1), 60–82. https://doi.org/10.1521/pedi.2010.24.1.60

Lavner, J. A., Lamkin, J., & Miller, J. D. (2015). Borderline personality disorder symptoms and newlyweds' observed communication, partner characteristics, and longitudinal marital outcomes. Journal of Abnormal Psychology, 124(4), 975–981.

Linehan, M., M., (2014). DBT Training Manual. New York, NY: The Guilford Press.

Luders, E., Toga, A. W., Lepore, N., & Gaser, C. (2009). The underlying anatomical correlates of long-term meditation: larger hippocampal and frontal volumes of gray matter. NeuroImage, 45(3), 672–678. https://doi.org/10.1016/j.neuroimage.2008.12.06

Lynch, T. R., & Cheavens, J. S. (2008). Dialectical behavior therapy for comorbid personality disorders. Journal of clinical psychology, 64(2), 154–167. https://doi.org/10.1002/jclp.20449

Mackereth, P. A., & Tomlinson, L. (2010). Progressive muscle relaxation: a remarkable tool for therapists and patients. Integrative Hypnotherapy, 82–96.

Martino, J., Pegg, J., & Frates, E. P. (2015). The Connection Prescription: Using the Power of Social Interactions and the Deep Desire for Connectedness to Empower Health and Wellness. American journal of lifestyle medicine, 11(6), 466–475. https://doi.org/10.1177/1559827615608788

Maslow, A. (1971). The farther reaches of human nature. New York: The Viking Press.

Matusiewicz, A. K., Hopwood, C. J., Banducci, A. N., & Lejuez, C. W. (2010). The effectiveness of cognitive behavioral therapy for personality disorders. The Psychiatric clinics of North America, 33(3), 657–685. https://doi.org/10.1016/j.psc.2010.04.007

McGinn L. K., & Young J. E. (1996). Schema-focused therapy. In P. M. Salkovskis (Ed.), Frontiers of cognitive therapy, 182–207. New York, NY: Guilford Press.

McMain, S., & Pos, A. E. (2007). Advances in psychotherapy of personality disorders: a research update. Current psychiatry reports, 9(1), 46–52.

Mhillaj, E., Morgese, M. G., Tucci, P., Bove, M., Schiavone, S., & Trabace, L. (2015). Effects of anabolic-androgens on brain reward function. Frontiers in neuroscience, 9, 295. https://doi.org/10.3389/fnins.2015.00295

Miller, C., Townsend, M., Day, N. & Grenyer, B. (2020). Measuring the shadows: A systematic review of chronic emptiness in borderline personality disorder. PloS one, 15 (7), e0233970

Paris, J. (2009). The treatment of borderline personality disorder: Implications of research on diagnosis, etiology, and outcome. Annual Review of Clinical Psychology, 5, 277–290.

Park, Lee & Imboden, John & Park, Thomas & Hulse, Stewart & Unger, H.. (1992). Giftedness and Psychological Abuse in Borderline Personality Disorder: Their Relevance to Genesis and Treatment. Journal of Personality Disorders. 6. 226-240.

Parra-Delgado, M., & Latorre-Postigo, J.M. (2013). Effectiveness of mindfulness-based cognitive therapy in the treatment of fibromyalgia: A randomized trial. Cognitive Therapy and Research, 37(5), 1015-1026. DOI: 10.1007/s10608-013-9538-z

Pec, O., Bob, P., Simek, J., & Raboch, J. (2018). Dissociative states in borderline personality disorder and their relationships to psychotropic medication. Neuropsychiatric disease and treatment, 14, 3253–3257. https://doi.org/10.2147/NDT.S179091

Ross C. A. (2007). Borderline personality disorder and dissociation. Journal of trauma & dissociation : the official journal of the International Society for the Study of Dissociation (ISSD), 8(1), 71–80. https://doi.org/10.1300/J229v08n01_05

Shearin, E. N. & Linehan, M. M. (1994). Dialectical behavior therapy for borderline personality disorder: Theoretical and empirical foundations. Acta Psychiatrica Scandinavica Supplementum, 379, 61-68.

Schulze, L., Schmahl, C., & Niedtfeld, I. (2016). Neural Correlates of Disturbed Emotion Processing in Borderline Personality Disorder: A Multimodal Meta-Analysis. Biological psychiatry, 79(2), 97–106. https://doi.org/10.1016/j.biopsych.2015.03.027

Schmidt, N. B., Richey, J. A., Zvolensky, M. J., & Maner, J. K. (2008). Exploring human freeze responses to a threat stressor. Journal of behavior therapy and experimental psychiatry, 39(3), 292–304. https://doi.org/10.1016/j.jbtep.2007.08.002

Stern BL, Yeomans FE. (2018). The Psychodynamic Treatment of Borderline Personality Disorder: An Introduction to Transference-Focused Psychotherapy. Psychiatric Clinics of North America, 41(2). 207-223.

Stiglmayr, C. E., Ebner-Priemer, U. W., Bretz, J., Behm, R., Mohse, M., Lammers, C. H., Anghelescu, I. G., Schmahl, C., Schlotz, W., Kleindienst, N., & Bohus, M. (2008). Dissociative symptoms are positively related to stress in borderline personality disorder. Acta psychiatrica Scandinavica, 117(2), 139–147. https://doi.org/10.1111/j.1600-0447.2007.01126.x

Stone, Michael & Hurt, Stephen & Stone, David. (1987). The PI 500: Long-term follow-up of borderline inpatients meeting DSM-III criteria I. Global outcome. Journal of Personality Disorders, 291-298.

Thompson, K. (2010). Therapeutic Journal Writing: An Introduction for Professionals. London, England: Jessica Kingsley Publishers.

Waldinger, R. J., Cohen, S., Schulz, M. S., Crowell, J. A. (2014). Security of attachment to spouses in late life: Concurrent and prospective links with cognitive and emotional well-being. Clinical Psychological Science, 3, 516–529.

Waldinger, R. J., & Schulz, M. S. (2010). What's love got to do with it? Social functioning, perceived health, and daily happiness in married octogenarians. Psychology and aging, 25(2), 422–431. https://doi.org/10.1037/a0019087

Yeomans, F. E., Clarkin, J. F., & Kernberg, O. F. (2015). Transference-focused psychotherapy for borderline personality disorder: A clinical guide. American Psychiatric Publishing, Inc..

Young, J.E.; Klosko, J.S.; Weishaar, M.E. (2003). Schema Therapy: New York, NY. Guilford Press.

Printed in Great Britain
by Amazon